AN INSIDER VIEW TO DOING BUSINESS IN MYANMAR

AN INSIDER VIEW TO DOING BUSINESS IN MYANMAR

Philip Zerrillo

Adina Wong

Singapore Management University, Singapore

NEW JERSEY · LONDON · SINGAPORE · BEIJING · SHANGHAI · HONG KONG · TAIPEI · CHENNAI · TOKYO

Published by

World Scientific Publishing Co. Pte. Ltd.
5 Toh Tuck Link, Singapore 596224
USA office: 27 Warren Street, Suite 401-402, Hackensack, NJ 07601
UK office: 57 Shelton Street, Covent Garden, London WC2H 9HE

British Library Cataloguing-in-Publication Data
A catalogue record for this book is available from the British Library.

AN INSIDER VIEW TO DOING BUSINESS IN MYANMAR

ISBN 978-981-124-002-7 (hardcover)
ISBN 978-981-124-003-4 (ebook for institutions)
ISBN 978-981-124-004-1 (ebook for individuals)

For any available supplementary material, please visit
https://www.worldscientific.com/worldscibooks/10.1142/12363#t=suppl

Desk Editor: Sandhya Venkatesh

Typeset by Stallion Press
Email: enquiries@stallionpress.com

Printed in Singapore

FOREWORD

25 years from now, Myanmar will not just be an Asian Tiger but an Asian Jaguar, an Asian Cheetah, because it's really sprung forward and taken lessons from all the other countries.

— Indra Nooyi, former Chairman and Chief Executive Officer, PepsiCo, USA, June 2013[1]

As Myanmar began to emerge from its five decades of military rule and international trade relations began to normalise, optimism was in abundance. National leaders at the 2013 World Economic Forum extolled the potential of this vast land mass that is rich with natural resources, a growing and underemployed labour force, and its strategic location among some of the world's largest and fastest growing economies and populations. That the potential is there was never in doubt among participants. Often speaking as a parent might talk about the potential of their child, speaker after speaker pointed to the macro indicators which would guide Myanmar to its rightful place in the future economy. However, just as parents know that a child will grow to a sturdy height and weight and gain a wisdom that will allow him or her to prosper, they are also aware that the future can dim if care is not taken to avoid the wrong path.

---

[1] Fujiko Takahashi, 'Top 10 quotes from Myanmar–World Economic Forum', *Thailand Business News*, 7 June 2013.

A new economy, such as Myanmar, does not come with a long and codified history of how to do business. Instead, the rules of commerce, property rights, financing and intellectual property are being created at a break-neck speed. While such laws, regulations and traditions are taken for granted in developed markets, they are a work in process in Myanmar and probably will remain so for the next several decades. Moreover, one often overlooks the need for skilled bureaucrats that can develop and evenly enforce rules. For a country transitioning from state-owned enterprises to a new 'market-based' commercial economy, the need for skilled bureaucrats could not be greater. Unfortunately, this is a process that takes time. While on any given day you can probably find 2,000 or more consultants and NGOs in Yangon ready to offer advice, the wheels of commerce are not yet turning effortlessly.

As we wrote this book, one of the fascinating insights we had was the frontier mentality that each of the entrepreneurs and commentators relayed to us. As local businesspeople wanting to help build a vibrant economy and bring better goods, services and employment to Myanmar, they were unable to wait for the rules of the road to become well-established and certain. Their futures are now, and the commercial roads must be navigated while being constructed. These daring souls have dived in, while international players have largely put a toe in the water as they look for low-hanging fruit to pick.

Beyond the rules of the road, a vibrant 21st century economy requires a skilled work force that enables the emerging businesses to press onto the frontiers of their industry. The capabilities, awareness and mindset of a workforce is a starting point for reconfiguring traditional industries, evaluating processes, and creating the need and awareness to change and transform.

Unfortunately, while many much-required structural changes have been identified and undertaken, the skilling of the workforce is a more difficult nut to crack. According to a World Bank report, agriculture's share of GDP declined from 52% to 32% between 2000 and 2015, while the share of manufacturing increased from 11 to 28%, and the share of services increased from 33 to 39%.[2] Despite these shifts, employment across sectors has remained fairly static: 52% in agriculture, 36% in services and 12% in industry.[3] Thus, as the economy goes through a fundamental transformation, the workforce is not keeping pace.

Today, most jobs are still in low-skilled occupations, with two out of every three workers engaged in low-skilled or subsistence agricultural work, which is categorised by the World Bank as the lowest paid and most informal type of work.[4] It is estimated that about 3% of jobs in Myanmar are classified as 'higher skilled'.[5] As we spoke with the entrepreneurs mentioned in this book, they commented that well-trained labour is in short supply. The workforce available has not experienced office, or even factory, work. And, as the businesses begin to grow, it was difficult to find talent that has experience with managing 20 or more people.

Developing this skill base will take time in Myanmar. The United Nations Children's Fund (UNICEF) reports that one in five Myanmar children do not complete primary education and less than 70% complete it on time.[6] With this sort of development pipeline, it

---

[2] The World Bank, 'Myanmar's Future Jobs: Embracing Modernity, September 2018', 12 October 2018.
[3] *Ibid*.
[4] *Ibid*.
[5] Naithy Cyriac, 'Myanmar Struggles to Build Skilled Workforce despite its Growing Young Population', YCP Solidiance, March 2018.
[6] *Ibid*.

creates a rather unusual challenge for labour policies. On the one hand, the domestic staff is not ready to assist in growing these businesses. On the other hand, it is difficult to justify permitting the highest paying jobs to be occupied by foreign talent. Many of the entrepreneurs we communicated with spoke passionately about encouraging the young expatriates who were living abroad to come home and do their part to build the new Myanmar.

As the country begins its journey of growth, the 'cheetah' has found the lack of infrastructure to be one of the most fundamental challenges facing the nation. The United Nations ESCAP in 2014 determined that Myanmar had the least developed infrastructure (telephony, transport, energy) in Southeast Asia.[7] Moreover, on a scale of 1 to 7, with 1 being the lowest level of infrastructure availability, Myanmar scored a 2.5 — well below the 4.5 world average.[8]

Power failures, a roadway system with less than 39% of the roads being paved, and the arrival of more cars, more transport and more traffic have begun to present new problems for the industry and the population. Moreover, as the consumer has begun to emerge and seek new goods and services from distant sources, the financial infrastructure has had to develop and at times leapfrog over traditional financial institutions and policies. As we interacted with the entrepreneurs featured in this book, we found that a number of them had confronted these challenges, and upon finding workable solutions, were able to develop businesses that could help others and be commercialised.

---

[7] Mr. Mathieu Verougstraete, UNESCAP Transport Division, Presentation to: Ministry of Economic Planning and Economic Development, 17 March 2017.
[8] World Economic Forum, Global Competitiveness Report 2014–2015.

To this day, there is a tremendous opportunity for those who can navigate the developing infrastructure challenges facing Myanmar. When the timing of transportation from the border crossing with Thailand (Mae-Sot) can vary from one to five days depending on the time of year and weather, global players find their supply chains, financial models, market information and operating procedures greatly challenged. It will take the assistance of these bold entrepreneurs to help turn the Myanmar dream into reality.

In the chapters and stories ahead, you will find some of the most ingenious, astute, passionate and adaptable people on this planet helping to raise the 'cheetah'. The opportunity for growth is certainly there — if and how it will happen are in the balance.

ABOUT THE AUTHORS

Authors

Dr. Philip Zerrillo is Professor of Marketing (Practice) at Singapore Management University, Singapore.

Adina Wong is Senior Assistant Director, Centre for Management Practice, at Singapore Management University, Singapore.

About the Editor

Dr. Havovi Joshi is Director, Centre for Management Practice, at Singapore Management University.

ACKNOWLEDGEMENTS

This book would not have been possible without the support of a number of people. We offer our sincere thanks and gratitude to the following organisations and people.

At the outset, we appreciate the support of the senior management at Singapore Management University. In particular, we would like to thank Professor Annie Koh and the Business Families Institute team for many of their introductions. Additionally, the SMU Office of Alumni Relations was instrumental in introducing us to many of the firms that we have chronicled in this book. We would also like to extend our special thanks to our colleagues at the Centre for Management Practice. In particular, we wish to acknowledge Michelle Lee Twan Gee, Sheila Wan and Irene Soh.

Special thanks go out to two SMU Alumni: Naing Ye Lin, for all the help he gave us in starting this project, and Evelyn Khin, for the assistance she provided in managing our day-to-day activities in Myanmar.

Last, but most important, to each of those sterling entrepreneurs featured herein, thank you for taking the time to share your stories with us. They were incredible, and we hope we did them justice.

Thank you.

Dr. Philip Zerrillo and Adina Wong

CONTENTS

Section 1

INFRASTRUCTURE

As Myanmar emerges from five decades of isolation, its progress will be shaped by the culture, history, ideas and institutions that are present in the country today. While the economy to date has been largely agriculture-based with limited skilled labour, it will need to transform rapidly to keep up with its neighbours and reach its potential. A key difference in developing today, as opposed to say 40 years earlier, is that Asia in itself has become a major consuming force. Thus, integration into the regional economy has become a more prudent path of late, rather than playing the role of Asian factory to the world. Indeed, the 2015 ASEAN Community pact stresses the need for political, economic and sociocultural integration. A lofty set of goals has been put forth, but development and integration do not happen overnight.

As we alluded to in our Foreword, many of the great challenges for Myanmar's emerging development path have to do with a lack of infrastructure. As Ma Cherry Trivedi, CEO, Myanmar Institute of Directors, points out, legal, governance, talent development and financial infrastructure are works in progress that continue to present obstacles. She says,

> *When we talk about the lack of infrastructure in emerging markets, we normally refer to physical facilities like transportation, energy and communications. In my opinion, Myanmar faces more of a critical shortfall in human infrastructure, which inhibits the country's ability to execute and implement its multitude of master plans and blueprints. No matter who is at the helm of a nation, leadership needs to bring in people who can actually execute. When there is a lack of relevant skills, regulations and legal enactments tend to be vague and often conflicting.[1]*

Retailing in an environment like Myanmar is not easy. As the market opened, there have been investments, even FDI, but they are not always equally distributed across the country. Rising incomes make retail a popular place for consumers to spend their newfound resources. However, retail is a down-stream business that depends on supply chains, government rules, coordinated processes and infrastructure to operate.

In the Keier group, we see a young dynamic and versatile company that is assisting local and foreign companies to overcome the infrastructure challenges they face. Whether it is office space, shipping, brand management, payroll, sales, document registrations or staffing, Keier is there to offer a helping hand. In a rapidly emerging landscape such as Myanmar, it is difficult for outsiders and locals to keep abreast of the changes and remain compliant. As international firms begin to dot the landscape of Myanmar, their goals are often driven by flawed top-down forecasts. A mineral rich country, with an under-employed labour force, experiencing new purchasing power and purchasing freedom, Myanmar seems an ideal market to enter during a quick analysis. However, as one

---

[1] Ma Cherry Trivedi, 'Doing business in Myanmar'. *Asian Management Insights*, Singapore Management University, 5 (2), 70–74, 2018.

begins to consider executing in such a market, stark differences begin to emerge. New entrants rapidly find that the strategies they are experienced in executing elsewhere are confined to a small segment of the Myanmar market. Through their provision of a broad range of services, Keier has proven to be well-poised to advise small and large firms alike.

Our next chapter on infrastructure is one that could easily be a consumer business as well. In Sithar coffee, we witness an entrepreneurial journey that began with putting coffee in the cup, and has then integrated backward into organising an entire agricultural sector. From its humble start making a few cups of coffee a day, Sithar is now advising farmers, working with various groups in Myanmar's conflict zones to provide economic choice, and trying to create awareness and demand for Myanmar coffee. A largely forgotten agricultural crop that has suffered from years of neglect, Sithar is building the agricultural blueprint to create a coffee industry, a reputation for the country, and opportunity for the farmers and their families. With the life and yield of a coffee plant exceeding 50 years, the effort they make today will be enjoyed by generations in the future.

Chapter 1

THE KEIER GROUP:
HAVE GAP, WILL SERVE

Myanmar is the last frontier. That is the reason why I, a Singaporean, came here. Because I know there are gaps here and I want to fill those gaps.

— Kenneth Tan, Executive Director, The Keier Group, Myanmar

The Keier Group is your go-to place in Myanmar.

This young, versatile group will provide for everything and anything that their corporate clients need. Its services include supplying serviced office spaces, deluxe serviced apartments, processing and distributing payroll, training their clients' sales agents and distributors, providing a full range of logistics services and conducting brand activation for their clients' brands in the tricky and rapidly emerging Myanmar marketplace. Seemingly nothing is beyond them, as they may be staging road shows, signing up new customers for their clients, handling sales for them, even going to the banks and running around to the ministries getting permits or simply giving them backup power. It even acquired vehicles for the ride hailing company Grab.

There is nothing and nowhere this resourceful group would not do or go to. Even if it means travelling to the most remote and inaccessible areas and waterways to tackle the most outrageous and unforgiving of assignments.

A Giant Hole in Office Space Supply

The Keier Group operates in two principal business segments in Myanmar: real estate (where it leases out serviced offices and serviced apartments) and logistics (wherein it offers services for nationwide distribution, import and export, warehousing and brand activation).

The seed of the group was first sown in 2012 by a husband and wife team of Chua Meimei and Kenneth Tan, both graduates from Singapore Management University, and their godbrother, Chervin Chow.

Formerly an Officer in the Defence Attaché Office to Myanmar, Singaporean Kenneth was in Myanmar because his Burmese wife was helming her family business. Chervin, a Singaporean, was a former investment banker with Lehman Brothers, now managing his family office C+S Global Holdings.

In 2011, Myanmar had just opened up its market. Coming in from out of the cold after decades of isolation, the country was introducing transformative economic and political reforms and companies were rushing in to check out the opportunities.

Foreign companies were eager to have a physical presence in Myanmar. However, they were finding it difficult to find suitable office spaces and living quarters for their foreign workers coming into Myanmar. The local business practice was to lease for 12 months, with rent prepaid for that period. That did not suit foreign companies; they did not want to commit for this long a term until they were on the ground and fully understood the lay of the land.

The trio saw an opportunity and responded by setting up Keier Business Centre in 2012, offering Myanmar's first ever fully furnished and comprehensively equipped co-working space for leases as short as three months.

At the time, the founding partners fancied themselves as the Regus of Myanmar (Regus is a global provider of serviced offices to clients on a contract basis). Recalled Kenneth,

> *Regus was trying to come in, but found it very hard to set up its business because there was no proper office space. There were office towers, but nobody was developing any office space. In short, nothing was available.*

Meeting Many Pressing Needs

The partners soon realised that the foreign corporations they were serving needed much more than a furnished office space. In the newly opened market, there were huge gaps in services everywhere in the economy — huge gaps that corporations could not leap over themselves because they lacked the local network and the local knowledge. Commented Kenneth,

> *Take my own case. When I first came here in 2009, I had trouble finding drivers and cars, getting money exchanged, and locating a corporate secretarial firm for my company. There's literally no help in Myanmar. You can't Google for information because the search results give you nothing useful for Myanmar. You have to actually go down to the ground to uncover the information. Or know a local who has the information.*

And even locals get caught out because things are in constant flux; one never knows when the government will discontinue a permit and the laws change every few months.

This state of general befuddlement parlayed into the unique role Keier would come to play in the budding local economy. Kenneth explained,

> *We saw gaps that made us realise that having a serviced office would help many companies because corporations come here with zero clue of what Myanmar is like. To fill these gaps, we began to offer a full suite of services including incorporation and tax advisory services.*

Keier promptly launched Myanmar's first-ever serviced offices. These fully furnished, well-equipped offices came complete with a comprehensive band of support services. The concept turned out to be a huge hit, landing Keier big-name clients like L'Oréal, Singtel and Expedia.

There was just one drawback: this business line was relatively easy to copy. Within two years, two competitors in the serviced office space popped up.

Keier's next business line, however, was not so easy to replicate.

Help Me Please!

Soon after its founding, it became clear to Keier that there were many more gaps that needed plugging as dazed and confused foreign companies floundered in the mishmash of broken roads, confusion, lack of transparency and red tape. The warehousing market had not developed, there were no trucking companies, the roads were not good, there were many rules, and all the rules were subject to arbitrary interpretations by local officials.

Keier responded by establishing Keier Logistics in 2016 to help foreign companies navigate the country logistically. Described Kenneth,

> For anybody who's looking to get in and open an office, it's really a maze. Because of that, people want more services all the time. Can you send this to here? Can you educate our team? Can you do brand activation? And we went, "Okay training, we can do that. Okay brand activation, we can do that...".

Keier Logistics was not any ordinary logistics firm.

Take Myanmar Apex Bank's rollout of its mobile banking platform in early 2016. The young private commercial bank was only one of a handful of private financial institutions in the country. Keier managed almost every facet of the launch. It recruited sales agents for the bank's comprehensive agency network, provided product training to the bank's agents, activated customers' accounts for the bank, and also staged roadshows to raise product awareness.

Or take the case of Grab. When Southeast Asia's leading on-demand transportation and mobile payments platform decided to enter Myanmar, it instructed Keier, 'We need to acquire taxis.' Keier's response was: 'No problem.' Grab went on to launch GrabTaxi in Yangon in 2017, and just one year later, it became the leading ride hailing player in the country. Said Kenneth, 'I'm proud to say most of Grab's taxis were acquired by us. In fact, you could say we helped Grab to be where they stand today in the country.'

By 2018, Keier Logistics' services included import and export services, logistics and warehousing, nationwide distribution coverage and brand activation. It offered clients local sales teams that covered permanent journey routes. It had warehouses in nine major cities in Myanmar. And its reach extended to 74 urban townships, 25,000 direct distributors and 20,000 wholesalers nationwide.

For the newcomer to Myanmar trying to dip a toehold into the emerging market, these services helped them hit the ground running. Perhaps more importantly, it could postpone the entering firm's initial capital expenditure until it had established a solid business model for the market. Keier's suite of services was designed to provide flexibility and turnkey operations.

Expansion into Serviced Apartments

In 2017, Keier plugged another gap by moving into serviced apartments. Keier's deluxe apartments offer full condominium facilities: such as a swimming pool, fitness centre, car parking and clubhouse, 24-hour security, fire alarm systems, private lobbies and earthquake provisions. Added Kenneth,

> *When expats come here, they don't just need an office, they need decent accommodation. By offering full-serviced residential properties, we wanted to enhance our services to our residential and commercial clients.*

In reality, Keier was reaping the full benefits of being a first mover.

> *We started very early and bought our properties at reasonable rates. So, our cost of doing business is manageable compared to our competitors who are coming in at this point in time. This allows us to be very competitive. Indeed, at all phases of*

our existence, we are way past the breakeven point; right from the start, we have been profitable.

For Keier's real estate competitors, the going was tougher. The pure play real estate firms bought properties at a time of rising realty prices and risked losses were their occupancy rate to fall below a certain level. And the opportunity for foreign entry was very limited as the waters around land titles and ownership were very murky in a nation that had typically always operated on a cash basis.

Local Insights and Bundling: The Basis of Differentiation

Kenneth explained,

Everything we do can be copied. The thing that is uniquely ours is the bundle of services we offer. It's all about the local insights that we possess and having the right things for our clients' needs.

Corporations don't come to us to just rent offices. They also have a need to understand the local dynamics. That, we are happy to share. This is a difficult market to navigate. If you don't speak the language, you will have to go through a lot of steps to get the different pieces of information you need, steps that include meeting the ministries and talking to them at so many different levels.

Keier essentially combined local Burmese knowledge with international business practices to provide the support that was adapted to local conditions and fit well with international clients. Said Kenneth,

I am a foreigner who is residing in Myanmar. I have both the local perspective and an understanding of how foreign

companies work. Because of that, we are able to be a bridge between Myanmar and foreign companies.

In for the Long Run

As of 2018, Keier was a lean organisation that was punching far above its weight.

The company had already been conferred a string of awards, including Best Serviced Office Development: Highly Commended (Myanmar Property Awards 2015), Best Residential Interior Design: Highly Commended (Myanmar Property Awards 2017) and Southeast Asia's Best of the Best Serviced Offices (Dot Property Group 2016). And, it had achieved all this with a staff strength of just over 20 personnel.

In the short term, many international players were looking at the Myanmar market as a place for rapid growth. Kenneth added,

> *One of the things we have to do is temper our customers' ambitions. Myanmar is a country that still faces many market challenges. Outside of Yangon, in places such as Mandalay, consumer purchasing power and transportation infrastructure are limited. Low purchasing power and a high cost to serve usually does not bode well for an importer, no matter how many people live there.*
>
> *Moreover, issues of reliability plague the economy and call for supply chain fixes that developed economies had dealt with 50 years ago. For instance, travel time for a truck from the Thai border crossing can take one day when the weather is good. When it is raining, it may take five days. Appropriate inventory stocking and the investment needed often make the Myanmar market less attractive than one might expect.*

For Keier though, it was just the beginning. Since 2012, Myanmar had witnessed tremendous growth. The partners believed that the country would continue to grow and that there was still great room for improved efficiency. And the Keier Group planned to grow with the country and supply the services that would make the future a reality. Said Kenneth,

> *We think we have staying power. Meimei is a local, and Chervin and I are localised Singaporeans, so I think we will always have more to offer the market given our collective network and experience. We plan to keep offering more services than our competitors. Ultimately, we want to be the number one player in the Myanmar market.*

For Keier, it was not just about making profit; it was also about providing employment for the Myanmar people and giving back to society. He added,

> *We've always been steered by our business vision and our values. We are a family business. And as a family business, we are anchored by values that we believe in, as well as the imperative to bring value to our clients. We want to be a forward-looking business that does things differently and positively impacts the community. We find our bearings based on how best we can contribute to the masses. We are always talking about how we can bring the cost down for the Myanmar consumer and make more quality products accessible to the people here.*

Upon final reflection, Meimei and Kenneth add, 'We want to help this country grow and for people to experience a better life. We want to build something good for this country.'

Chapter 2

SITHAR COFFEE — GROWING THE COFFEE INDUSTRY IN MYANMAR

There are many things I want to do for the company and the country. But one company cannot do this alone.

— Thu Zaw, CEO of Sithar

Sithar Coffee started out in 1996 as a simple coffeehouse selling premium specialty coffee to local Myanmar customers. Run by Tin Tin Win, it began operations with one to two customers a day. In slightly more than 20 years, the company has integrated its business into the entire coffee value chain — from growing coffee, and ensuring peaceful harvesting and distribution of rural coffee production to providing services to coffee retailers.

Thu Zaw, CEO of Sithar, took over the family business in 2016. He did not choose the easiest path for building his business. The growth that he envisioned involved the company venturing into areas of great uncertainty — going upstream to plant crops. While entrepreneurs, investors and financial advisors typically want to reduce the financial resources committed to a project, Thu Zaw invested in and attempted to develop the supply chain from the growing of the bean to the time it reaches the consumer's cup. Going beyond a coffee shop to try to develop an integrated coffee industry created an opportunity to provide a social good, and a sustainable agricultural community that could span multiple generations and build around the brand of Myanmar coffee. Through Thu Zaw's leadership, the company extended its activities to touch all elements of the value chain in bringing coffee to the consumer.

Coffee was first introduced to Myanmar in 1885 by British colonists, when missionaries set up small farms in and near Pyin Oo Lwin (about 65 kilometres east of Mandalay). However, the industry did not take off for nearly a half century. While it was an ideal place to grow it, Myanmar was little known for its exotic beans. This provided both a challenge and an opportunity.

Starting with a Coffee Shop

Sithar's history began with a coffeehouse. In 1996, Thu Zaw's mother, Tin Tin Win, opened a coffee shop selling premium coffee. Commented Thu Zaw, 'At that time in the '90s, when the country started to open up, there wasn't a proper coffee shop in Myanmar.'

The coffee shop was named Fuji Coffee, a Japanese name, because the coffee was brewed with beans imported from Japan. The beans were roasted in a small manual roaster with a small electric motor. Thu Zaw described the kind of environment his mother wanted to create with the café,

> In a city where there weren't proper hotels, it wasn't easy to find a place where businesspeople could meet and talk, or families could spend time in. The café provided a proper setting, in a comfortable neighbourhood, where these people could come.
>
> But in those days, serving one coffee cup for about 500 kyat (US$0.30) was really quite expensive. We were selling

one to two cups a day, and anyone looking at our business thought we were crazy.

Upstream and Downstream

While Sithar had started off importing specialty coffee for the niche premium coffee segment, it gradually expanded to importing beans for the commercial and organic coffee segments. It stuck to its guns on sourcing its own coffee beans, drying, roasting and grinding them at its manufacturing sites to produce unique flavours. Sithar decided against going into the freeze-dried soluble coffee segment, which was prevalent in neighbouring Vietnam. Thu Zaw explained,

There are two markets in coffee. One is soluble coffee, which is instant coffee. The other is our segment of roasted coffee beans. A lot of the coffee companies here today will bring in roasted coffee powder in bulk, repackage it, blend it with a non-dairy cream and sugar, and redistribute it again as instant coffee.

Sharing the motivation to go into upstream coffee planting, Thu Zaw said,

Coffee is the second most commonly traded commodity of the world. A lot of foreign investors, including many private equity investors, are more interested in the downstream businesses where the quick money is. Roasting and supplying beans give you a higher return on investment. Our cash cow is in the steps between the farm and the coffee shop, as we convert the harvested beans into unique offerings for our business and retail clients. But we still have to devote some resources to developing further upstream, too, because we cannot forget that while down-stream may be expanding, people will also need to grow coffee to ensure sufficient supply in the long run. Investment in the source of beans is very cash-intensive. And it is not a one-company solution.

Expanding into the Value Chain

From importing coffee beans, Sithar turned towards cultivating its own coffee plantations in regions such as Pyin Oo Lwin, in northeast Myanmar. Thu Zaw explained,

Besides importing coffee beans, we also run our own plantations, but our philosophy is not to do everything by ourselves. There's no point of owning everything; we have to share it. We believe very strongly in community involvement.

Sithar encouraged farmers in the community to grow coffee by giving them seeds, facilitating the transfer of agricultural technology, and providing funding. Besides investing funds into the growing and processing of coffee beans, Sithar went further to provide buyback guarantees to the farmers to ensure that their coffee beans, when harvested, would be sold. Such guarantees provided the security of income in future years, which encouraged farmers to invest in upgrading their perennial coffee shrubs that had begun to face declining yields during the prolonged isolation of Myanmar. Thu Zaw commented,

Growing a perennial crop like coffee needs to be managed with a long-term perspective. There are two varieties typically grown in coffee, Arabica and Robusta. In Myanmar, we grow mainly Arabica and these plants are still young; however, the stock of Robusta is getting old after years of

underinvestment. When a coffee seed is planted, it takes about three years before it starts to bear fruit. And after 50–60 years, it starts to reach maturity and needs to be replaced. Reinvesting in their fields has always been a difficult decision for the farmers, as the Myanmar market was typically plagued by great economic and legal uncertainty. In addition, coffee price volatility is high. The farmers also need intercrops, or other crops to sustain them. So we encourage people to focus not just on coffee, but to grow other crops, too, for a more stable cash flow.

However, education and encouragement are needed for the farmers to want to plant coffee seriously. Thu Zaw added,

On paper, we have about seven to eight thousand metric tons of coffee per year. But there is probably a gap with the actual output. People sometimes just want to own the land that has been set aside for planting coffee. They may not have a real passion or the business model to grow coffee. They may not really be growing or optimising their crop yield. Plants could be ageing or having low yields, or the fruits could be dropping and there is a lack of infrastructure to harvest and process them. The beans are just being wasted.

We have a very close-knit partnership with our communities, and today [2018], we supply products to the entire retail industry — distributing to food service companies, hotels, restaurants and coffee shops in 45 cities around the country.

Exporting Coffee

Sithar had sister companies that traded Sithar's coffee beans in the market. In fact, up to 30 percent of Sithar's coffee harvest was supplied to other coffee roasters.

While the domestic market experienced double-digit growth, Sithar also exported a small quantity of its coffee to the US and Europe (mainly Russia and Denmark), Asia (Japan, Korea, Thailand, Malaysia), and Australia. 'For export, I would say we don't follow the diaspora. Only a very small percentage of the generation of Myanmar people who had migrated overseas are quality coffee drinkers. We sell more to countries where we have good business relations; what we would call "relationship coffee",' said Thu Zaw.

He also elaborated on the importance of having a unique proposition for Myanmar coffee,

> We have to position ourselves differently because we don't have the scale, processing capabilities, logistical infrastructure, farm-to-market roads or mechanisation in our agricultural sector to create a competitive price advantage. We've got competition from Vietnam, Laos and China. Marketing well with a compelling and different story is key for us. We really have to promote well and have strong relations with our distributors and partners around the world.

To help the farmers sell their crop, especially for export, Sithar also provided them credit. He explained,

> While exporting is a good thing, farmers don't understand the logistics involved, and may not have the liquidity needed to complete the export process. Once the coffee arrives in, say, the US, there is a quality check before the cash can be transferred back. This can take several months, and somebody has to be able to absorb that need for liquidity.

Sithar — The Second Generation

Thu Zaw had spent several years working and studying outside Myanmar before returning to run Sithar in 2016. By then, he had already chalked up a number of years of extensive experience in the corporate world, namely in petrochemical and commodities trading.

As he was the second generation of leaders for Sithar, by the time he assumed the helm of the company, parts of the infrastructure were already in place: the plantation, roasting facilities and distribution network had been started. Upon taking over the running of the business, Thu Zaw refined the business model to bring the company 'to the next level'.

In the two and a half years since he started running the business, Thu Zaw had focused on three key areas: prioritising customer service, offering a one-stop solution to customers and cultivating coffee in the conflict zones.

Prioritising Customer Service

The focus was on prioritising the customer through better outreach and customer service. Sithar expanded its distribution network, opened more showrooms and staffed its stores with more manpower. Thu Zaw noted that businesses tended to be sales-oriented, but he wanted Sithar to be differentiated through its attitude towards service. He said,

> *Anybody can serve up the same product, but being service-oriented is more important than being sales-oriented. Providing excellent service is very different from selling. We are very strong in after-sales service — machine maintenance, training, certification, customisation of coffee blends.*

Thu Zaw recognised that the customer experience depended primarily on the people they interacted with at Sithar,

> *People are our most important assets and I ensure that I train my people well. We bring in world-renowned*

> *talent — world champions, world celebrities who are*
> *internationally certified — to train my people. Yet, we also*
> *open these training opportunities to other stakeholders in*
> *the coffee industry, so that they can also learn with us.*

The world-class training that Sithar provided for its staff has also enabled them to take part in international barista and latte art competitions.

Offering a One-stop Solution to Customers

Sithar concentrated on offering its business-to-business customers a one-stop, turnkey solution for their coffee needs. This ranged from providing basic coffee beans to a distinct coffee blend that helped them differentiate their menu. Sithar also provided the machinery and equipment for clients to brew and distribute coffee in their shops, and to have staff available for servicing whenever the machines broke down or needed maintenance (so that coffee sales could continue on the same day). Thu Zaw was pleased with the result of the approach,

> *The hotels, restaurants and the rest of the coffee industry*
> *really respect us for that. That's our competitive advantage —*
> *customisation and service. No other local coffee company*
> *in the area is like us in terms of quality and service*
> *approach.*

One of the barriers to wide acceptance of ground and brewed coffee was the machinery required to produce the beverage. By Myanmar standards, coffee machines were a significant capital investment for the local food and beverage retailer. To take customer service a step further and enable the industry to advance, Sithar also provided credit to their customers, as purchasing a coffee machine was often out of the question, forcing the retailer to shift to cheap instant options. Thu Zaw explained,

We're currently doing the financing by ourselves with our own cash flow. This is again, a capital-intensive undertaking on our part, but a necessity to drive the industry. But, fortunately, one bank is willing to do it with us soon.

Cultivating Coffee in Conflict Zones

Thu Zaw was very focused in terms of what he wanted to achieve through the expansion of Sithar's coffee-growing capacity. 'When I took over the company, we had only one plantation. We had existing infrastructure, but I wanted to think differently about growth going forward,' he said.

To produce more varieties of coffee, and at scale, Sithar did not face many, or any, formal competitors. Farming cooperatives were weak in Myanmar. Yet, there were other obstacles to production. Thu Zaw was pushing for coffee to be cultivated in the Golden Triangle region in Myanmar (the Golden Triangle spanned Myanmar, Laos and Thailand), commonly known for the growing of opium crops. He wanted farmers to replace illicit crops with coffee as a cash crop as a viable alternative to facilitate eradication of the opium trade. 'My focal point today for growing coffee is in the conflict zones. In the Golden Triangle communities, we can use coffee to create a livelihood of peace,' said Thu Zaw.

He also wanted to provide jobs to soldiers and internationally displaced persons from the conflict areas during peacetime. After developing new areas for coffee plantations to create jobs, Sithar further subsidised its coffee bean sales to coffee shops. Thu Zaw recognised that he was in a unique position to support these communities, as the conflict zones engendered a level of uncertainty that foreign direct investors would prefer to avoid. 'This is an area where a lot of external investors may not be able to reach, or, even if they could, they may not be able to navigate successfully. There's no certainty; it's a grey area. There's no solid legitimate way to deal with those regions,' he said.

Because working in these communities was a very sensitive task, cultivating trust with the farmers was key in bringing about change. Even agencies like UNODC (United Nations Office on Drugs and Crime) could not easily reach out to the parties living in the local communities. Thu Zaw explained,

> There has to be trust and understanding, but I've worked with many NGOs in this country, and sometimes as a private sector company, we also need them. But within each institution, people will have different interests, and you really have to navigate a maze to get their understanding and move in the same direction. And NGOs are sometimes only focused on the short term. They are given a grant for a five-year project cycle, and are focused on delivering certain outcomes during that time, after which they leave. There's no sustainability for the project after that, and we are unable to maximise the potential of the initiatives undertaken. Whereas we are demonstrating every day that we will be here for the long haul.

A Country Vision for the Coffee Industry

With an understanding of the local coffee landscape, as well as a personal vision for Sithar and developing the coffee industry in Myanmar, Thu Zaw has stepped easily into the role of a private sector leader working with the government to formulate a strategy for the local coffee industry. This comprised working with other private enterprises and coffee associations, as well as liaising with the government to discuss how the coffee industry could be developed and determine the target quantity of coffee that should be grown. In effect, Thu Zaw helped to develop a 10- or 20-year vision for the country's coffee strategy.

He explained the importance of public sector partnerships in developing the coffee industry,

> *Myanmar is currently a relatively small coffee producer; it has no economies of scale. Coffee production is expensive and the costs to doing business are high. Because of superior logistics infrastructure outside Myanmar, very often somebody who has the equipment and the machinery, and the other factors of production, can produce at scale outside the country, and then bring coffee into Myanmar much more cheaply than he/she is able to produce here.*

Defining Success and Looking Ahead

Thu Zaw recalled what his mother's vision was for Sithar when she first started the business,

> *She believed in good quality and sophistication, which is why she started the coffee shop. It was her home, where she could invite and entertain guests and show them the best hospitality. She also wanted to give people a good cup of coffee, something distinct that they would enjoy. She was already very satisfied and happy to be able to provide that. My vision is different in the sense that I have a more expanded view, and a more global outreach.*

What were the key milestones ahead that Thu Zaw wanted to achieve in his pursuit of success? There were a few pieces that would complete the picture of Sithar that he had in mind.

Firstly, it was about what he called 'consolidating the tangible and intangible values in the company', and he elaborated,

> *There are things of value that you can measure, money and operating performance, but there are also intangible assets, such as relationships and reputation, that are important and need to be fostered.*
>
> *Intangible assets also include building the capacity of Sithar's people. If we're going to enter global supply chains, our coffee has to meet the international standards of lab testing, such as having a limited number of contaminants and meeting agricultural specifications. Our farmers will need training so that they're not using the wrong chemicals and pesticides — coffee beans are porous, which means that they will absorb virtually anything. So, we need to bring in the right people to do research in many areas, such as food science. Further downstream, barista training will be very important to strengthen the image of our quality of coffee.*
>
> *We're also extending our service in agriculture. We're tapping into the communities and growing coffee. It takes a lot of resources, getting NGOs, banks or foreign institutions involved and, especially, patience.*

Secondly, maintaining sustainable growth meant making tough choices. Given his personal objectives to deal in the conflict zones, Thu Zaw was careful about choosing suitable sources of funding. He said,

> *Money is important, but we also don't want to accept it too easily. Once you accept money from certain investors, you have to meet certain conditions. As my outreach today is in the conflict areas, I don't want those constraints. The*

scorecards change every day; someone who is a friend today might be on a blacklist tomorrow. The last thing I would want is some of these international organisations dictating, in a country where relationships are long term, who we can or cannot do business with. You have to be able to sit across a table, look at each other eye-to-eye and be trustworthy. So being selective about the source of funding is one constraint to growing as fast as I would like.

Thirdly, while the winds seemed to be blowing in Sithar's favour and the overall consumer demand and the marketplace seemed to be growing, the company needed to continue to develop both its downstream and upstream relationships. Thu Zaw would have to continue to work closely with the government to plan the coffee growing roadmap and craft a robust agricultural policy towards coffee going forward. But, to remain relevant in the market, he would also need to understand the growing and rapidly emerging segments of the nation's coffee culture.

Fourthly, as it developed new areas of cultivation for coffee, Sithar would have to develop the ability to grow and process coffee locally at scale, to lower cost and be more competitive with international brands on the international market for exports, as well as in the domestic market.

Finally, Sithar wanted to raise consumer awareness about the heritage of Myanmar coffee, which has yet to gain international awareness as a place for esteemed coffee.

Thu Zaw concluded, 'I'm always working 24/7, and there are many agendas for me. Sithar is bringing its own resources to the table to achieve them, but there are areas where we cannot do it alone.'

Creating an ecosystem is not an easy nor an overnight process, but then social, economic and cultural change rarely is. Sithar's management team is the kind of entrepreneurs that a developing economy needs. Focused on peace, prosperity and building a better reputation for Myanmar agriculture, Sithar is a long-term player with a long-term vision.

Section 2

THE CONSUMER

This is Burma, and it will be quite unlike any land you know about.

— Rudyard Kipling, Nobel Prize laureate, 1898

To understand Myanmar's current and future consumer, it is important to look back in time, and understand where we are and how we got there. The Myanmar consumer is emerging from a long slumber that lasted over five decades. Faced with limited product and service options offered by state-run enterprises and monopolies, the Myanmar consumer was, on the one hand, a do-it-yourself producer, who made what was needed and perhaps offered a surplus to the local market, and on the other hand, one who has been ingenious at sourcing goods via informal grey and even black markets.

In 1960, Myanmar was thought to be one of the countries with the brightest economic future in Asia. With a literacy rate in the top 50 worldwide, Myanmar was ahead of Korea, Taiwan, Malaysia, Thailand and China, as well many other of today's most modern societies.[1] In 1960, the average income of Myanmar was triple that

---

[1] Norton Ginsburg, 'Atlas of Economic Development', 1961.

of Indonesia, and more than twice that of Thailand.[2] Indeed the consumer economy was growing, and the future was bright.

In 1965, the United Nations famously predicted that Myanmar, the Philippines and Sri Lanka would be Asia's next tigers. Each held a top two position in the global export of rice, sugar and coconuts, and tea, respectively.[3] However, none of these countries realised that destiny. Instead, each took a prolonged detour during which domestic production and consumer options were severely limited. But today, the Myanmar consumer is waking up to a new reality and a new marketplace.

As the consumer becomes reengaged in Myanmar, many international players have struggled to understand the market, the consumers' needs and their expectations. Indeed, there is limited commercially collected market research and consumer insight available. What information has been available has pointed broadly to increased purchasing power, the advent of international imports, and a need for quality at an affordable price. Havas Riverorchid, a market research firm in the Mekong region, reports that the Myanmar consumers are experiencing 'a new kind of fear — the newness that comes from letting the world in as borderless communications and smart phone technologies now provide information access like never before.'[4] Winning the consumers' trust in your products and services, as well as providing clear instructions, is hence key, since it provides you with a competitive advantage.

---

[2] Peter Coclanis, 'Asia's Next Tigers? Burma, the Philippines, and Sri Lanka'. *Journal of World Affairs*, 175 (6), 2013.
[3] *Ibid*.
[4] Santiphong Pimolsaengsuriya, 'Ten consumer mega-trends in Myanmar'. *The Nation Thailand*, 21 June 2016.

While this has been a challenge for some time, the young consumers are beginning to jump in. As they do, these emerging purchasers are demanding beauty at a reasonable price, products that have personal purpose rather than head-turning appeal, and provide good value for money.[5]

For this book, we had the opportunity to meet with entrepreneurs who are deriving their insights and forging into the market with new goods and services. During the interviews we conducted, perhaps the most gratifying and sound justification for new and improved services we heard from the entrepreneurs was to 'improve the lives of the Myanmar people,' and to 'preserve our heritage and traditions and make products that suit the Myanmar people.'

In the following chapters, the reader will have a chance to look at Tree Food and Bella Cosmetics — two companies with a similar heart, working at opposite ends of Myanmar's heritage. In the case of Tree Food, Cho Lei Aung, the founder, has attempted to rejuvenate demand for a traditional Myanmar after-dinner sweet by adapting it to the consumers' lifestyle, improving product consistency and artistically delivering it to the end consumer. The traditional brown sugar jaggery sweet, made from the sap of palm trees, is abundantly available in Myanmar. However, the younger generation and the emerging consumers were largely ignoring the product. It wasn't exciting, and was packaged in large chunks, which are considered too large to be consumed anywhere except at the family home. Quality varied greatly, and as a locally produced product available in abundance, no one had really thought about how to package it and offer a greater variety. Medically trained, art- and fashion-inspired, it took an entrepreneur

---

[5] *Ibid.*

like Lei Aung to rethink the production, packaging, flavours and product consistency. Today, her artistic packages, in new and unique flavours, can be found in upscale and artisan shops in Mandalay and Yangon.

In Bella Cosmetics, we see an intense desire to bring beauty and style to the Myanmar woman, to protect the local consumers from harmful counterfeit products, and to create makeup that is suitable for the earthy tones of the Myanmar woman, all at a reasonable price point. CEO and founder Wai Thit Lwin takes the reader through a journey of her discovery of the intricacies of makeup and the near avoidance of it by Myanmar women. Her insights as to why and how women use makeup, their value points, and the future plans of Bella provide a glimpse into the modernising Myanmar consumer.

Peace Myanmar Group is a fascinating story of how three college friends, Tun Linn, Thein Win and Min Aung, came together to develop a safe product of global standards. Current Group General Manager Ei Phyo tells the story of how these three entrepreneurs met in college, created a product, and then had to go door to door to sell it. Beginning with rum as its initial product, by 2018, the Group produced a broad line of spirits and beverages including drinking water in eco-friendly containers, and boasted of annual sales of over 12 million bottles of rum alone.

In the case of Yankin Kyay-Oh, or YKKO, as it is known today, Aye Myat Maw, the Director (Marketing and Business Development), YKKO, explains how one of Myanmar's largest restaurant chains has grown from a single restaurant begun by her parents and her aunt and uncle in the family home to a multi-location operation employing over 1,500 people across Myanmar's major urban locations. Beginning with a simple desire to bring traditional

Kyay-oh soup to their neighbourhood and treat the customers as though they were guests at home, by 2018 YKKO boasted of more than 30 locations. As Aye Myat Maw describes, running the business has not always been easy, and transitioning to a second generation of management has been a challenge. But by keeping the customer first, they have been able to successfully navigate the food and beverage landscape.

The final company in this section is a story of a father and daughter who came together to develop a personal care company, Beauty Palace, which is giving even the largest multinationals a run for their money. Chua Meimei, Board Director of United Beauty Palace Myanmar, relates the rise from a limited line of soap products to the launch of top selling toothpastes, antibacterial soaps and shampoos. As a local player, she has relied upon her market insights and familiarity with the habits of Myanmar families as she builds brands that not only compete in the big cities but also dominate the countryside. She details the company's ambitions to be an internationally recognised global player.

Chapter 3

TREE FOOD: MODERNISING TRADITIONAL BURMESE FOOD

I want to bring traditional products to people in a modern way. And the modern way is in different sizes, different packaging, different recipes and different ways of eating.

— Cho Lei Aung, Founder of Tree Food

If you walk down the aisles of one of Myanmar's top food retailers, you may notice the artistically packaged jaggery products produced by Tree Food Co. Ltd. Still a business of limited scale, trendy consumers are searching out the Tree Food products in Yangon. From the hand-designed and often handmade packages to the traditional Burmese food product of jaggery, or brown sugar made from the sap of the palm tree, Tree Food is capturing the tastes and interests of locals and foreigners alike. Begun in the family kitchens and conceptualised on an artistic easel, this three-year-old company is selling more than 5,000 products every month. Its founder, Cho Lei Aung, is just getting started.

Sprouting the Idea for Tree Food

Lei Aung was an unlikely person to start a business, much less a consumer food company. She had graduated from Jinan University in China with a degree in medicine. Despite her qualifications, she decided to pursue other interests, and explained,

> *I knew that I was not going to be a doctor. However, because we have a lot of difficulty with education here, when you go to the big cities and are asked what you want to be, you choose to go to medical school because your family wants you to receive a good education. So I went to medical school. After I graduated, I decided not to go into the medical profession. I started a tailor shop, making clothes with my sister. We just started in a storage room of my sister's house. She knew how to make clothes and I helped her in marketing. Our dream was to create a fashion brand, with our own design and our own distribution. But the fashion brand failed to take off.*

The exposure to fashion and design while running the tailor shop stirred Lei Aung's creative side. She continued to explore her artistic desires and took up painting, becoming the student of a well-known female artist in Myanmar. As Lei Aung learnt more about art from her teacher, she felt that she wanted to be an artist, too. However, as it would be difficult to survive as an artist in Myanmar, she decided against it. Nevertheless, she was still kept awake by the idea of combining things that were artistic and related to painting, as well as her own background in medicine and experience running a small business. As Ralph Waldo Emerson wrote, 'The mind once expanded has a difficult time regaining its original shape.' The sum of Lei Aung's experiences had equipped her for a rather unexpected commercial and cultural journey.

She decided to focus on something to do with food. 'Food is very interesting. Food has colour, texture, appearance and different combinations of colour and various combinations of flavours.'

Jaggery itself is unrefined sugar, which makes it healthier than processed white cane sugar.' Lei Aung decided to devote her time and energy, and exercise her talents and interests, into experimenting with food. But the idea for Tree Food only came about slightly after she began her foray down this path.

The Idea of Tree Food Takes Root

In Myanmar, one could find a lot of imported foods and snacks that were colourful and delicious — in fact, a local could almost forget about the Burmese traditional foods. Lei Aung decided to research the market, and began to pay more attention to the products she encountered and the way they were delivered.

> One day, I went to a traditional Burmese restaurant. After the meal, they give us a piece of jaggery, served in the traditional way, in large chunks. It was much too big a piece for a daytime, after-meal snack. I thought — the pace of life changes, and lifestyles change over time, but the food has stayed the same as during my grandpa's time. Why don't we change the design of the jaggery snack to meet the needs of the times... from a large piece to smaller bite-sized pieces? And then I started thinking about producing small pieces of jaggery in packages that were just enough for one-time consumption.

With that idea, Tree Food was born at the end of 2015.

Crystallising the Basic Idea

To start making the jaggery in small batches took Lei Aung a year of research. While it was easy to find jaggery in the local wet market, which was sold in bits and pieces at very cheap prices, Lei Aung noticed that the quality of this jaggery was usually very low and varied greatly.

> If the quality is low, then it's not that interesting any more. I wanted to create a 'Made in Myanmar' food product in a way that people could remember it as a high-quality product... In Myanmar, the general standard of food safety and quality is very low. I wanted to showcase our local products in the best possible way. So, the idea for my company was about making traditional food in a modern and innovative way.

Lei Aung went to talk to the farmers who produced the jaggery in large batches. They were unwilling to help her produce a small quantity of jaggery in the small pieces she wanted, because it was highly labour-intensive. So Lei Aung eventually bought the large-sized jaggery from the farmers and cooked it to her own specifications in her home kitchen (which could accommodate four people). Tree Food's inaugural product was ready for launch.

Modernising Traditional Jaggery

Lei Aung targeted the younger generation for her products, as she believed that they would like to try new experiences and products. Youthful segments the world over tended to seek the greatest variety. Her idea was that this younger generation would buy her jaggery and share it with their families at home, which in turn would spread the news about this product through word of mouth. It was like bringing a message home to remind the family members of their own childhood when they used to snack on traditional jaggery. But being a little different and in smaller bites, it was both interesting and easy to try.

To market her new products, Lei Aung initially went to art shows to sell them. 'I just quietly put my jaggery at the reception area. I tried... and I failed a lot of times. I succeeded in making the small bite-sized pieces that I envisioned, but I felt that it was still not interesting enough to entice people to purchase.'

Lei Aung had to find a way to make the jaggery offering more attractive for buyers.

While at the supermarket, Lei Aung perused the shelves and came upon the chocolate section, where she hit upon some inspiration.

> I looked at the chocolate on display. Chocolate comes in various flavours and a myriad of packaging and size options. And then I thought that chocolate has a lot of external value rather than just eating it — because chocolate is also used to express love. We also say that we eat chocolate for the love of it. Jaggery too is sweet, so why can't it be used to represent some sweet values as well?
>
> I then started to add flavours to the jaggery. In the beginning, I experimented with menthol, and then green tea. Now we have four main flavours — yogurt, plum masala, tamarind, and ginger. Ginger is healthier because the jaggery can be dissolved in hot water to make ginger tea. And in the same way, we can make tamarind juice with the jaggery pieces.

Getting Off the Ground

With the four key flavours, Lei Aung also crafted jars and bottles to package the products. In her first year of business, she would buy a small quantity of glass jars, and make her own labels for them.

'I did all the artwork — creating the logo, hand drawing and printing the labels, packing the bottles,' she said. The different flavours and handcrafted packaging helped Lei Aung market her products on Facebook to customers.

In the first few months of business, Lei Aung would sell about 100 to 200 bottles of jaggery a month. In good months that figure would reach 500 bottles. Describing how labour-intensive the business was in the start, she said, 'I drew the labels for every bottle. Because in 2015 and 2016, it was very difficult to find packaging materials in Myanmar. And then the printing. The printer wanted me to print at least 1,000 pieces, but I did not need so many.' Indeed, that would have been many months of labels for the products.

On the back of the packages, Lei Aung would print a description of the jaggery product, explaining how it was made and that it was a traditional Burmese snack:

"Htaann-Lyet", Product of Myanmar 100% Handmade

Toddy Palm Jaggery (Htaann-Lyet) is the Myanmar traditional sweet, to serve as dessert after meals to aid digestion. It is a popular snack in the country. It is rich in iron, other minerals and vitamins. Jaggery typically comes from the sap of toddy palm trees that grow in tropical environments, especially in central Myanmar. The art of making good jaggery lies in climbing very high trees and tapping them to extract sap. The collected sap is then boiled to evaporation and balls of jaggery are made from the syrup.

Tree food is a contemporary twist of jaggery, natural extracts, powders and other natural ingredients by own homemade recipes with health benefits. There are no preservatives and artificial ingredients.

Fast Forward

Following up on her original intent to create different recipes for traditional Burmese food, Lei Aung came up with a new range of products at the end of 2017, including a tea leaf pesto. She elaborated,

> *In Burmese olden days, we'd eat tea leaf salad. It was something you would enjoy, but it wasn't paired or integrated into any particular dining experience. When I went to the United States in 2016, I saw dishes such as olive pesto that you would eat with crackers and cheese, and it would be paired with a glass of wine. So I thought, if we want to increase the demand for tea leaf to help the farmers, then we should create a different way of eating it.*

Lei Aung explained that the tea leaf pesto was produced as a sauce in a bottle, and was made with cashew nuts, sunflower oil and a pinch of salt. There were three flavours — original, curry and basil. 'Usually tea leaf is eaten with beans and rice and accompanied with a cup of tea. But, this one is more for sprinkling on pizza. And then having it with wine.'

By 2018, instead of hand-painting her packaging in very small quantities, Lei Aung used standardised and ornate packaging for her seven stock keeping units (SKUs) of products. She sold about 5,000 packets of jaggery a month, while the tea leaf products were in the early stage of marketing and promotion.

Additionally, in the early days she sold her products solely via Facebook, but by 2018 they were available in more than 40 City Mart supermarket outlets citywide.

Interest in Tree Food has certainly grown compared to the early days. 'I think in Myanmar the trend is starting to change. Everyone is interested in learning more about Tree Food, and the media is coming and asking about me, my story and how it began,' said Lei Aung.

Production

High-quality raw materials were an essential part of ensuring the quality of the final product. Lei Aung partnered with 15 farmers, who supplied Tree Food with the jaggery for cooking. Through her relationships and the climate of trust and common purpose she had established, she was able to source better jaggery than one would traditionally get in the wet market. She added,

> *We cannot say that the jaggery is organic, because we don't also have a certificate, and it costs $1,000 an acre to certify your crop and get one. But we care about the cleanliness, hygiene, and product quality. It is very hard to deal with the farmers and ensure consistent quality without trust. And, [she emphasises] that has to be built over time.*
>
> *I used to have thousands of small suppliers, who I don't use any more, because the jaggery they provided was of very bad quality. I had to throw away a lot of the product in the beginning. But now I have a very good relationship with my suppliers, and we are slowly improving the relationship day by day. I also have a main supplier, who is helping to manage everything at the production facility.*

Growing the Team

As demand for Tree Food products grew, Lei Aung also hired people to grow her team capacity.

She had four people working in the kitchen, cooking the jaggery and tea leaf and packaging it, as well as a driver for distribution.

While Lei Aung hired a freelance accountant, she mostly took care of the marketing, finance and HR activities herself. 'My sister sometimes helps me with some of the financing and HR and other tasks, because I also need to make trips to the city.'

Growth was financed initially with money from the tailoring business, and also some loans from her family.

Challenges

While the business had grown steadily, there were ongoing challenges that Lei Aung found herself having to grapple with.

The daily expenses involved in running the business were very high. She explained,

> *Myanmar can be a very difficult place to work in, if we really want to work in an absolutely ethical and legal manner. Taxation and other expenses are also really high. For example, I am going to open my own production facility soon, but I don't own land yet. So I have to rent land at a very high price. Even when there is a business downturn, rent stays expensive. And, I have to learn how to handle things like arranging for water and electricity, which are often unavailable at critical times. There are a lot of additional costs.*

In addition, Tree Food products were positioned as a kind of luxury product that was considered expensive for middle and lower-middle income consumers.

The weather and erratic supply of raw materials were other issues to be dealt with. Lei Aung elaborated,

> *Because jaggery comes naturally from trees, it depends a lot on the weather. Too much rain is not okay, and no rain is also not okay. If that happens, prices are going to climb a lot in the coming year. Availability is also seasonal. I need to have a storage system, as the jaggery season lasts six to eight months in a year, and it can be stored for a maximum of four to five months. So I have to be very diligent.*

The final key challenge was related to packaging. As readymade packaging was not easily available in Myanmar, Lei Aung had to source materials from Thailand, China and even as far as Indonesia. 'There are also a lot of risks that we have to take when we order from overseas. But all my packaging materials, from the bottles to the paper bags and boxes, are imported,' she said.

Future Plans

In Search of New Heroes

Where does the future take Lei Aung? She is hugely interested in new product development — creating new things.

> *In the future, I'm going to do more projects, with the advice of some mentors. My strategy is to produce new products in small batches. I will then test them out in the market. It's like a betting game with small stakes; a game that I will play over and over again. For the products that don't make it, I will scrap the idea. For those that catch on with consumers, the so-called heroes, I will add them to my product range.*

Apart from product expansion, Lei Aung would also like to take Tree Food overseas. She and a few partners had been trying for two years to produce their own supply of jaggery from palm nectar. The finishing touches were in the process of being put on at her new production facility, after which Tree Food would be ready to produce on a very different scale. 'In the kitchen, I can produce five gallons worth of jaggery a month. But with the factory, we are talking of two tonnes a month, which means I can scale up to 10,000 units a month. And, my new factory is going to do all of the cooking, cleaning, and packaging,' she said.

Growing Tree Food

Lei Aung had considered many factors in determining how Tree Food's expansion plans would proceed, and explained,

> Because of the politics and business conditions here, sometimes it's easier to focus on expanding to foreign countries. But it doesn't work well sometimes, like in European countries where they can sanction very quickly.
> The other risk is that there isn't much spending power locally, so we have to produce a cheaper product. So I would like to produce a cheaper product made with natural fruit, and start selling this in the local market by the end of 2018. I do have a local audience, who is excited about the 'made in Myanmar' proposition. It's like starting a revolution and creating hope for the next generation.

It has to be Something You Enjoy Doing

Looking back at the business, which was barely three years old, Lei Aung took note of how her role had changed over time.

> At the beginning I had a lot of fun, and there was little pressure because then things were just starting up and I had not invested much capital. It is fun to make something and have people say, 'I like it.' I would play around with the product, the packaging design and branding depending on

what worked and what didn't. And I also experimented with different ways of marketing on Facebook.

    Now we're running on more capital and it's harder to grow to the next level. Now it's not quite as fun any more. Because I have to handle a lot of things at the same time. And with the additional sourcing capability, all of a sudden you have to manage raw materials, and you have to manage people coming to work, and you have to manage inventories and stocks. You have customers, and you don't know when they will order and how much they will order. There are a lot of calculations and estimations that just go on and on.

Lei Aung paused at these sobering thoughts.

While at the beginning I just played the entrepreneur, doing whatever I wanted, now I'm trying to be systematic and put things into standard operating procedures (SOPs) and policies. And this is where I always envy painters, right? They paint something. Then they hang it up, and people bid or pay for it. And that's it!

Moving to a certain level of scale requires many decisions — not all of which are easy to make for one trying to preserve and reenergise a nation's culinary roots. In the early days, as the entrepreneur tests the market and receives responses, changes can be made quickly as SOPs, customised requests and variety can be accommodated at a low cost. Eventually, there are demands for consistency and repeatability as customer expectations are established and expectations need to be met. Such is often the case when the artist entrepreneur begins to grow their enterprise. The intense desire to keep the artistic DNA of Tree Foods, as the firm tries to satisfy a loyal and growing customer base, has been evident in the creation of new products, packaging and routes to market.

Tree Food is a one of those companies that is preserving the precious heritage of Myanmar, albeit in a modern form. In doing so, it is preserving the essential characteristics of a traditional food product and adapting it to a new format for new generations in modern society — thus ensuring that this heritage stays alive and close to the minds and hearts of the locals.

Chapter 4

BELLA COSMETICS: TRANSFORMING A NATION THROUGH BEAUTY AND CONFIDENCE

I want to add confidence to the women and men of Myanmar. If they're more confident, if they're more capable, then our country can be different. I think, that's the way I can show my love for my country most.

— Wai Thit Lwin, CEO of Bella

Bella Cosmetics was the biggest makeup brand for women in Myanmar in 2018. Its most popular cushion foundation sold 300,000 units a month on average. Wai Thit Lwin, CEO of Bella, had started the business only 18 months earlier. How did she garner so much success in such a short time? Sometimes inspiration is born from the most unusual of insights.

Trained for Business Since Young

Reminiscing about what she did after school and on weekends, Wai Thit recounted,

I didn't decide to be in business, but I was trained by my father since I was seven years old. He made me do book-keeping at his warehouses. Well, I thought I was doing it,

> *but actually somebody else was at it! But, parents can trick*
> *you into thinking that you're the one doing it.*

At the age of nine, Wai Thit's father began to introduce her to the different departments in his company — the showroom and the service centre, marketing, accounting and others, for a period of three to six months each.

> *He started me with cleaning, because he said that's all I was*
> *qualified to do. So, I had to clean his office and the office*
> *around it, and I got to eavesdrop on everything that was*
> *happening. I sometimes think you can learn an awful lot*
> *about a company with a broom and good ears!*

Wai Thit's father ran a number of different businesses, such as movie production houses and construction companies, hotels and plastic factories, but the main line of his business was consumer electronics. He was the sole distributor of Sony products in Myanmar. This was a relationship that had lasted for almost 30 years. From the age of 9–15, Wai Thit was put in charge of small projects in some of these companies. In 2002 (when she was 15), she was asked to help her father launch Sony's Cyber Shots and Sony Ericsson — which she did, and effectively headed.

Upon graduating from high school in Myanmar in 2006, Wai Thit went to the US and earned her undergraduate degree in business at the University of California, Berkeley. 'While at Berkeley, I suggested to my father that we should start something on our own, because my father was then the sole distributor for both Sony and LG.' That was in 2006–2007, when the first wave of original equipment manufacturer (OEM) TVs came into Myanmar, becoming the TV of choice for Burmese households (instead of Korea-made TVs). Her father then started a company with his own brand of electronics, T. Home. Wai Thit was in charge of the brand marketing.

In order to do this while at university, she had to conduct frequent conference calls on Skype and Google, and send numerous emails after school. She also visited Myanmar four times a year.

Coming Back to Myanmar

Wai Thit returned to Myanmar from Berkeley in 2009, graduating in just three years, a year ahead of her class.

> *I came back primarily because I was engaged to be married. Plus my father was saying, "You have to come back and take over the family businesses. I've been training you for this your whole life." But when I got back, he said, "The electronics business is a very stable business. If you want to prove your skill, then you need to run the construction materials business", which is what we were just starting.*

So Wai Thit ran the family's construction and materials business. Within three months, she had tripled its sales. Next, under Wai Thit's suggestion, the family bought a ceramic tile factory. It took about a year to get the factory running. Within a few years, Wai Thit increased its market share, and upped the turnover by about six times.

Wai Thit's husband was a serial entrepreneur with businesses in many industries. Subsequently, when he started a hospital, named Victoria Hospital, with a friend, Wai Thit started working part-time for both her family businesses — the construction material company, and her husband's hospital. She worked at full throttle all the way to the birth of her elder daughter,

> *The hospital was going to open its doors 45 days after my elder daughter's birth. On the day of my delivery, I went from my office at the hospital to the delivery room, and*

I delivered the baby at 12pm. My first meeting after that was at 5pm. And then I worked from my birthing suite, and went back to work full-time on the tenth day.

In 2011, US sanctions on Myanmar were lifted, and in 2012, the hospital was sold as the removal of sanctions had opened up several new opportunities in the country. 'And our key strength is that we are, in the end, marketers,' Wai Thit added.

After selling the hospital, Wai Thit's husband asked for her help to run the ABC chain of convenience stores, which he had started in 2006. She did this for four years. Wai Thit said of her husband, 'He likes to start businesses. So I would run it with a COO, and then I would hand it over to the COO, who became the CEO once the business was stable. That's how we functioned. In the group, we have around 30 CEOs taking care of 30 different businesses.'

Given the multiple hats she wore to run the various businesses, Wai Thit had to exercise very creative time management skills to juggle her roles as a businesswoman and mother. She explained,

I wake up at 6am. I'm a mother from 6am to 8am. My kids go to school at 8am. I go to meetings for my first business from 8am to 12pm. Meetings for my second business are from 12pm to 4pm. And then, when my kids were younger, I would go home at 4pm, spend time with them from 4pm to 6pm. They would start eating at 6pm, and then their Chinese tutor would arrive. After 7pm is playtime. So from 6pm to 9pm, I would have another bunch of meetings at home. And then from 9pm to midnight, I had my last series of meetings for the day.

In 2014, Wai Thit's father had to undergo a series of surgeries. She took over the running of the family businesses during this time — until 2016, when her father recovered. She then handed the company reins back to him.

Personal Care and Makeup

In March 2016, Wai Thit got to thinking. ABC convenience stores was running smoothly, and her father was back at the helm of the family businesses. She had started to free up some time and wanted to do something on her own, which was not about helping her father or husband run their businesses. She recalled laughingly, 'I wanted to finally do something before my husband comes up with another idea and throws something new at me.'

Wai Thit's motivation for a business idea sprung from the values that her great-grandfather had imparted to her. It was important for her family, which was relatively well-to-do in Myanmar, to serve their fellow citizens and help them improve their lives, as only then would the country improve. This desire to see her countrymen improve their lives dovetailed with another separate incident that ignited Wai Thit's idea for her own business. In 2016, on the day she had to attend a gala, she had forgotten to book a makeup artist. Left to her own devices, it dawned on Wai Thit that she had no idea how to put on makeup. Even though her dress designer offered to help her, Wai Thit decided to find out more about makeup on her own.

> So I watched all of the makeup tutorials on YouTube by celebrity makeup bloggers, such as Jaclyn Hill, Jamie Page and Kathleen Lights. And I was amazed. It was like a whole new world — makeup!

Wai Thit started wearing makeup to the office, and people started to take notice. 'I found that people appreciate it if you put in some effort. When I received compliments, it boosted my mood and I felt more confident and energised to do more, which, in turn, makes the business better.'

A Market for Makeup

Wai Thit started asking around as to why people were not wearing makeup, and three main answers came back.

The first was that they simply did not know how to.

Related to this was the second reason, which had to do with the unaffordability of makeup products for the average Burmese woman. In 2016, typical drugstore brands were twice as expensive in Myanmar as compared to Singapore. Also, as monthly salaries in Myanmar were around US$100, the average woman would find paying US$10 for makeup extremely expensive. What was more, these international brands would rarely be the latest products launched by the brands, and were often not fresh stock by the time they arrived for sale in the Burmese market. For Burmese women who wanted to wear such makeup, the choice was expensive or stale makeup, or worse, fakes. Wai Thit explained,

> *What women could afford was around US$5 to US$7, but they could not buy quality makeup with that. And the only substitutes are fakes. It breaks my heart, because women wear makeup to be pretty. If you wear fake makeup, your face will get destroyed because of all of the mercury and steroids that they put in it.*

The third reason was that the cosmetic shades made by international cosmetic brands were simply not suitable for Burmese women.

Most of the Asian cosmetics aimed to whiten the skin. But, with the deep rich skin colour of the Burmese woman, these imported brands made the women look pale, like ghosts. What Wai Thit and her team recognised was that the Myanmar market needed cosmetics that worked with the darker skin tones of the Burmese to bring out their radiance.

While producing the right products, modestly priced and of high quality standards was the starting point, Wai Thit knew that access to the consumer would be critical. But this final point was her strength — she had spent her life gaining access to consumers all over Myanmar — this was where she truly excelled.

Bella Cosmetics

In 2012, a Korean conglomerate, and one of the biggest Korean cosmetics manufacturers, asked Wai Thit if she would like to distribute some of their cosmetics as they wished to enter the Myanmar market. Although it was a timely opportunity, Wai Thit turned it down, knowing that Korean cosmetics would sell at a price that was unaffordable for Burmese women. Moreover, Myanmar was not the right climate for the Korean-made makeup. As Korea could get very cold, most of the makeup and skincare produced there were suitable for colder climates. Myanmar, though, was very hot and humid. Additionally, Burmese women had a golden undertone to their skin, whereas Korean makeup was based off either pink or yellow skin tones. Wai Thit declared, 'I believe that makeup helps you enhance what you already have. It's not to make you another person. You have to be yourself, but better, and more confident.'

Wai Thit believed that Myanmar women, in general, were capable and had an inner-strength. However, they would often prioritise their husbands and children before themselves. By the time their children were grown up, they had forgotten who they were and lost confidence in themselves. Wai Thit said, 'I want to tell Myanmar women: 'You can achieve your full potential'. That's what I want to give them, confidence to be successful.'

Wai Thit believed that marketing existing products was not the way to achieve her goal of providing makeup that was suitable for Burmese women. She wanted to bring out their natural beauty, and address the factors relating to their skin undertone, oily skin type and humid weather. 'If you cannot create something, you can only market what is available. If you can create something, you can create solutions for the whole group.'

Collaborating with Cosmax

This insight led to her decision to create Bella cosmetics. Wai Thit researched and found that Cosmax, based out of Korea, was the biggest cosmetics OEM in the world. However, Cosmax did not respond to Wai Thit's initial emails. So Wai Thit did what she had to do to speak to them — in May 2016, she 'stalked' the company to the Shanghai beauty show, one of the largest beauty shows in the region. It was the only beauty show that Cosmax participated in (in Asia), and they had the biggest booth at the show. There she met Hana Kim, who was in charge of Cosmax's international sales. Coming from LA herself, Hana connected well with Wai Thit. Commented Wai Thit on their conversation, 'You see this girl who's dressed in slacks, who speaks very good English, and has a proper business plan, and everything. But you've never heard of Burma. Why would you trust somebody like that? But she did.'

In June 2016, two weeks after the show, Hana made a trip to Myanmar. Wai Thit recalled,

Cosmax at that time had said to Hana, 'No, you cannot expand to Burma because it's a scary place. Why would you go there?' But she believed in me. So Cosmax began to produce my products... And it has been a great fit for us. It was a full-fledged facility that produced all types of skincare, colour cosmetics and personal care. Working with them, we felt like we knew the whole family from the start.

The relationship with Cosmax was a close one, with the management of both companies sharing closely aligned values. Wai Thit elaborated,

I know their entire management. They know me. We work like a team. We have an agreement and a contract that I will not work with anyone except them. And they will not work with anyone in Myanmar except me. We have exclusives. In the end what it comes down to is the relationship and the trust.

Cosmax sent some researchers to Myanmar to conduct tests and help with product development to come up with Bella's first product, which would be suitable for Burmese women and Burmese weather. It was a 'cushion' format-liquid makeup and a sponge, in a compact. Wai Thit said, 'We also have skincare inside because people in Burma don't wear skincare. It's waterproof, because it rains five months a year in Myanmar.'

The cushion makeup suited the local conditions perfectly. It had a matte finish, so that the face would not look shiny in humid weather. The formula also contained sunscreen, Spf50+++, to protect against the harsh tropical Burmese sun, and had tints that reflected the golden Burmese skin tone. Like all subsequent Bella products, the cushion makeup was waterproof and smudge proof, to stay securely on the face.

Cosmax not only worked hand in hand with Wai Thit to design the Bella products, but also worked on projects outside of the business. The Cosmax chairman and Wai Thit engaged in charity work together. To commemorate the second anniversary of their working relationship, they were building a school in Myanmar, opening in October 2018, which would provide education to 800 children annually.

Launching Bella Cosmetics

Bella Cosmetics was finally launched in October 2016. It was an instant success with the Burmese women, with 50,000 cushions selling in two days. Wai Thit said, 'Now, we are selling one cushion every 10 seconds.' Items in the Bella product range were priced at US$7 or less, to be affordable for the average Burmese woman earning US$100 a month. Foundations cost US$4, and lipsticks at US$2 each. Other related items such as makeup remover and masks were priced between US$2–3. Wai Thit explained, 'It all adds up to about US$7. No woman wants to buy just one thing. You would want to buy at least two to three of the lipsticks, or an eyebrow pencil.'

Bella was affordable compared to the international drugstore brands because it was designed to be that way. Wai Thit ensured that her products were manufactured with affordable packing, and while the drugstore brands would charge about ten times the cost, Bella charged just enough to cover its overall costs. 'Colour cosmetics is all about packaging and the margins are crazy. I just want to break even after spending on marketing'. She added, 'But no one can fight us on quality.'

Marketing

In a country where people rarely wore makeup and even fewer knew how to, Wai Thit had to figure out how to encourage people to wear makeup daily, and also teach them how to wear it correctly.

A traditional marketing approach was used to gain awareness as Bella began advertising on television. In Myanmar, celebrities such as actresses were huge motivators to encourage people to follow their actions. Until recent years, there was hardly any makeup advertising on state-run television. Wai Thit worked with different popular Burmese actresses to create beauty tutorials and TV programmes on how to put on makeup. These actresses would appear on TV, saying, 'Don't I look pretty?' This was the first time all of these actresses would be seen together on a large scale, as part of a marketing campaign. 'We had to educate the masses through actresses. That gets people very interested, and women now start to say, "I want to wear makeup",' she said.

Besides relying on celebrity endorsements, in 2017 Bella sponsored the equivalent of the Myanmar Oscars, a high-profile event that made Bella Cosmetics known to the nation. In 2018, targeting Bella's male customers, Wai Thit signed an agreement for Bella to be the main sponsor for English Premier League Broadcasting and World Cup Broadcasting in Myanmar.

Bella also had a large presence on social media. Observed Wai Thit,

The bigger part of our marketing is via social media. We're probably the most active Facebook page in Myanmar. We have around three to four million engagements daily. We get around 5,000 messages and around 5,000–6,000 comments every day.

Wai Thit also hired professional help to develop an app for would-be Bella users. The app would help those new to cosmetics to choose the right product to use. The users could take a picture of themselves using the app, which would then diagnose the user's facial characteristics, such as face shape and complexion, and recommend suitable Bella products to use.

Reception

The commercial reception for Bella was better than good. People liked the product so much that they would even wear the makeup to sleep.

However, with this popularity also came some incipient problems. 'We launched a waterproof product, but we didn't realise that people did not know how to clean it off,' said Wai Thit. While in the beginning people loved the product, the assumption was that they knew how to practice a proper cleaning process to remove the makeup. After two weeks, without proper cleaning, people started having breakouts... And the comments spilled onto social media. 'I got this cushion, it's so bad. Selling at a cheap price, it's very low quality.' Starting from a base with limited category knowledge and low purchasing power, it only made sense that the consumers would try to wear the makeup a little longer, and perhaps not know how to properly clean it off.

Addressing this problem was a delicate issue at best, explained Wai Thit,

> When I say to someone, "Please clean your face", they react very negatively, shooting back, "Oh, you're telling me that I don't clean my face. You're saying that I'm dirty." My response is, "No, I mean, please clean your face properly.

You need to do double cleansing. You need to exfoliate every other day. Only then your skin will be good. And if not, don't wear makeup. Just do cleansing every day and wear sunscreen. But even if you wear waterproof sunscreen, you have to clean that off, or it will clog your pores and you will get a breakout." But people get very offended if you say that. So I've had a lot of personal attacks.

To address this problem, Bella provided a complete solution. For example, in the cushion makeup tutorials, there was a segment at the end that reminded people to clean their face after applying makeup. Bella would also run simple campaigns with the tagline, 'Let's wash our face'. Of course, there remained a small percentage of users, around two to five percent, who were allergic to makeup.

Product Range and Identity

My sincere wish is for every Burmese to be beautiful and confident.

The first range of Bella Cosmetics focused on getting the basic formula and colour right for Burmese women to start wearing makeup daily. Besides the cushion, the makeup range had a foundation powder pack and loose powder. For skincare, there were soothing gels, mists, facial wash and sleeping masks.

In late 2016, Wai Thit wanted to incorporate the idea of Burmese national identity into her second range of makeup — this would be the Thanaka collection, a product extension made of Thanaka. Thanaka was produced from the pulverised bark of certain trees like sandalwood, which were found abundantly in Myanmar. Applying Thanaka, in the form of a white paste, across their cheeks and foreheads, was a long-used method by Burmese women to protect and beautify their faces. Thanaka was also supposed to have a whitening and sun protection effect.

In developing the Thanaka makeup series, Wai Thit wanted to reflect the natural properties of Thanaka as an astringent, antiseptic, antifungal, sun protection, anti-ageing cosmetic. Thanaka cushion makeup had six key properties: it cooled the skin, offered sun protection, had a refreshing smell (like natural Thanaka), oil control, whitening, and liquid to powder with sustainable production. Wai Thit elaborated on the sustainable aspect of Thanaka,

> *As natural resources go, teak is very rare now. So are rubies. If we keep digging for them, they will be gone. It is the same for jade. I want everybody to know about Burmese Thanaka, something sustainable that Myanmar could be known for.*

In October 2017, Wai Thit launched a second line of makeup, which was conceptualised by her two daughters — Hearty Heart. This line of makeup was aimed at the tweens and teenagers.

Wai Thit explained why it was important to design a collection for tweens that they could call their own,

> *If you are a teen, you don't want to use makeup that your mother uses. I never used Estee Lauder until now, because my grandmother used that. When I went to college, I started using MAC and Bobbi Brown. And then my mom said, 'Oh, it's good. Let me start using it.' So you don't want to use what your mother used — your mother wants to use what you use. It's the opposite. You do want her bags, and her shoes, and her clothes if they are back in fashion, but you don't want to use the same cosmetics as her.*

The Hearty Heart line was named by Wai Thit's elder daughter. Its logo consisted of two hearts: a pink heart to represent the elder daughter, and a yellow heart to represent the younger daughter, who liked the colour yellow. The first Hearty Heart collection was called the 'Ice-Cream Collection', because both daughters were 'obsessed' with ice-cream. Even the makeup was perfumed to smell like ice-cream. 'Bella doesn't have this because it is more of a serious makeup brand. This is meant to be a fun makeup brand.' The tag line 'cute and fun' represented what Wai Thit wanted the brand to be for everyone — cute like her elder daughter, and to have lots of fun like her younger one.

Distribution and Manufacturing

I want to produce something that my daughters and I would wear. All my products are paraben- and cruelty-free.

Part of Bella's success was owed to a healthy distribution network. Thanks to the distribution capabilities set up by Wai Thit's husband's businesses, Bella could be found directly and indirectly in about 200,000 stores throughout Myanmar. 'They go to fast-moving consumer goods (FMCG) outlets, cosmetic outlets, as well as modern trade outlets. I could grow this business quickly because of our experience in FMCG distribution.' Bella also had about 50,000 stores of its own in Myanmar.

While demand and distribution were in place, manufacturing had to scurry to catch up. With Cosmax already running at full capacity before Wai Thit formed their partnership to produce Bella Cosmetics, a new solution had to be found.

Cosmax asked me if I wanted a factory in Myanmar — but I could not afford that. Mainly because I couldn't afford the manpower to manage 200 researchers — visas, importing raw materials... and I would have to be the one responsible for all the electricity, which is difficult in Burma. So then they said, 'Where do you want it? Vietnam or Thailand?' I said Thailand, because it's closest to Burma. So they now have a factory in Bangkok.

The Bangkok factory opened in May 2018 manufactured for Bella and focused on the Southeast Asian market.

Wai Thit was strict on manufacturing quality control. Third-party testing for every batch of product was conducted in Singapore, the US continent, Poland, Korea and Australia.

I concentrate on what I'm good at, which is choosing the right products, making the right product for the Burmese, and marketing it, and making sure that people can use it, and people learn how to use it. So I don't want to have to worry about the manufacturing problems.

Looking Ahead

With the supply side settled, Wai Thit was looking ahead at growth.

In 2018, Bella launched a range of skincare products. While developing makeup was mostly about getting the colour and pigmentation right, skincare was a bit trickier. She explained,

Launching skincare in a country that doesn't have any knowledge about skincare is not easy; it was not possible to just create a product that everybody would easily adopt. Because the skincare line was based on the cost, it took a long time to actually develop it. And then we tested every-where. Blind testing alone, which took place in various countries overseas, took three months.

Another new range that Wai Thit planned to launch was Bella's men's skincare line. 'What scares me now is that with the men's line, I'm going head to head with all the multinationals. They have much deeper pockets than I do. I'm doing this just to build confidence for my people. This is my social business.'

With a view to regionalisation, Bella would launch in Thailand later in 2018, once supply was ramped up. Wai Thit wanted Bella cosmetics to be available to Burmese expats living in Thailand. 'In Thailand, there are Burmese who cannot afford Thai makeup. So I want to sell to Thai Burmese at the very affordable price that we sell in Burma.' The launch of Bella in Thailand would also mark the premiere of the Thanaka line for the international market, where products would be sold on Amazon as well. 'In this worldwide economy with e-commerce, everything is made easier.'

As Bella had been manufacturing to international standards, it was well-poised to sell its products to international markets.

Having come thus far with a long runway ahead to cover, Wai Thit reflected on her current team's strengths, 'We have around 60 people in marketing and social media, product design and product testing. 400 people in distribution.'

Was Wai Thit having fun running Bella?

As the management team was assembling for a meeting outside the conference room, Wai Thit smiled broadly as she shook her head backward; *I was here until 2am last night with the whole management team, and then I came back to work this morning at 9am to meet you and talk about the company.*

I enjoy seeing people pretty and it's sustainable. So my happiness now comes from reading people's comments on Facebook saying that, 'Oh, finally I can afford to use something that is good. It is a very good product that is very worth it. Thank you.'

It's not about numbers any more. It's about creating happiness and confidence.

With happiness and confidence, and a bit of style and grace, Bella Cosmetics is building the confidence of consumers as they engage in the new workplace that has begun to characterise Myanmar. As the cities bustle, and media exposes people to more fashion and art, Bella is helping to provide convenient, safe and affordable beauty made for the Myanmar consumer.

Chapter 5

PEACE MYANMAR GROUP — BRINGING QUALITY BEVERAGES TO MYANMAR

We want to innovate and bring beverages of international standard to Myanmar.

— Ei Phyo, General Manager of Peace Myanmar Group

Peace Myanmar Group (PMG) had its beginnings in one product — Myanmar Rum — being sold by its three co-founders walking around the city selling door-to-door with their backpacks in 1993. By 2018, it was a multimillion-dollar business, selling about one million cases of rum a year (or roughly in excess of 12 million bottles), among other beverage lines that it offered.

While the start of the business had both serendipitous and thorny beginnings, its vision and mission have always been a clear and strong driving force for the co-founders.

A Chance Start

PMG, a home-grown Burmese beverage company, produced both alcoholic and non-alcoholic drinks. It was best known for its 'Myanmar' brand of alcohol, namely, Myanmar Rum, Myanmar Dry Gin and Myanmar Whisky.

PMG was founded in 1993 by three friends — one of whom was Ei Phyo's father, Tun Linn — along with Thein Win and Min Aung. Tun Linn met his co-founders at university, where they became close friends, sharing very similar backgrounds and dreams. They came from small towns in the Delta region, Ayeyarwady, and moved to Yangon to become entrepreneurs. Tun Linn was in the paints business and had been since the 1980s. Another co-founder was in the textile manufacturing business, and the third was in rice trading. The three would hang out at Tun Lin's paint shop whenever they were free, and when Myanmar started to open up in the mid-1990s and regulations became more business-friendly, they decided to work together to start a business.

Back then, the beverage industry, and especially alcohol, like many others, was tightly controlled by the government. Being a predominantly Buddhist country, the government also wanted to limit the quantity of alcohol that people consumed. There was only one brand of rum in the market, Mandalay Rum, which was produced by a state-owned enterprise. The problem was that the singularity of this rum spawned many counterfeits and knockoffs in the black market, as its flavour was easily replicable. However, this illicit market was next to impossible for the government to regulate, and many people who drank these low-quality knockoffs became sick, and some even died from drinking them.

Realising that the black market had burgeoned into a collection of illicit and illegally produced variety of products, the government responded by privatising many of these sectors and industries, and then selecting who it wanted to give the production licenses to as a means to control quality. Alcohol was one of the products in the consumer food and beverage industry to be privatised.

The three friends saw an opportunity in consumer goods, specifically in beverages, to create quality products at an affordable price for the Myanmar consumers. Putting their heads together, they initially wanted to start a business manufacturing soft drinks. However, they faced difficulties in obtaining the relevant government licences, and so were 'pushed' into exploring the alcohol space, where the government gave them approval to operate. It was actually a huge risk to take to enter this industry, as none of them came from any kind of distilling or manufacturing background — they were just small town boys who had moved to the 'big city' to see if they could make it.

Setting Up the Business

The three friends travelled to various countries to put together the knowhow they needed to assemble their distillery. Ei Phyo commented, 'They had to set up everything from scratch on their own. For example, they went to India for distilling columns and boilers, to Scotland to learn the actual process of distilling rum, and to the US for the casks and learning the process of ageing the rum.'

In 1993, there was only one type of alcohol that was prevalent in Myanmar, and that was rum. And within that, the government-produced Mandalay Rum was practically the only one available. Though share data was not available, in the authentic spirits market it was nearly a complete monopoly as there were virtually no imports at the time. Beyond it, only cheap knockoffs of Mandalay Rum were present in the market.

Fresh from their trip around the world, the founders were inspired by the Scottish distilleries that were hundreds of years old. How could they also build a company for the long run, and what products should they make? The founders knew that if they tried to become just another knockoff product, making rum of a similar or lower quality to Mandalay Rum at a discount, they would not be able to build a sustainable business. Differentiation was needed, and quality and integrity were the keys. Fighting it out with the government brand or the illegal counterfeiters was not a route that they wanted to take.

To come up with their first product and flagship rum, they carefully tested multiple rum flavours before zeroing in on what they felt was the best bet to produce — a flavour that the market grew to accept and finally love. This rum became the flagship product for PMG — Myanmar Rum. Over time, the Myanmar label expanded to include whiskey and dry gin. And while there has been product proliferation, 'Rum is our founding product and still is our best seller to this day,' said Ei Phyo.

Finding its Legs

Besides being a new brand, the company faced other problems in operations. While many companies worked closely with the military government, the PMG founders decided to stay away from mixing business with politics. This modus operandi not only limited the growth rate of the company, but also created operational challenges. In the early years, PMG cars and sales team were stopped at the border of the Shan State, where one of their competitors had a close relationship with the local authorities. 'The border guard would stop any company car, would hold up a Myanmar Rum bottle and say that if you are a car that's carrying Myanmar Rum, you are not allowed in, or you will be jailed,' said Ei Phyo. This was an example of some of the initial challenges that the founders at PMG had to work with.

The first year, PMG struggled to sell 6,000 cases of rum (one case comprised 12 large bottles). Ei Phyo added, 'Currently, we are selling more than one million cases a year.' As of 2018, the PMG beverages comprised two main product groups: alcohol and bottled drinking water. Starting from Myanmar Rum, the Myanmar brand was extended to Myanmar Dry Gin and Myanmar Whiskey. The company also started a manufacturing plant for bottled drinking water, marketed under the brand name Myanmar Drinking Water.

Market Evolution

Tun Linn had seen the market evolve over the decades with PMG. In the beginning, alcohol was very much a seller's market. Ei Phyo explained,

> The early days were the golden days where you could sell almost any product you made. Because supply had been so limited, the market was able to absorb all of the new entrants that entered.
>
> The government still restricts the number of players in the industry today, because we're a Buddhist country, and it doesn't want alcohol abuse. So, it limited the number of alcohol licenses, which are very specific-purpose licenses.
>
> You need a license for each step of the alcohol-making process. I can have the distilling and the storage licences, but if I don't have the bottling licence, then I cannot bottle my alcohol. The government has very stringent regulations, but it can also be favourable because that means high barriers to entry for new players.

By 2018, there were more local players, but the government limited the number of alcohol imports from foreign competitors. It was, however, common for neighbourhood stores to sell illegally imported alcohol as the borders with the neighbouring countries were relatively porous. For example, a lot of beer from Thailand flowed into Myanmar each year.

The trend for consumption was shifting towards whiskey, and Grand Royal Group, a local Myanmar Producer founded in 1995, was the biggest player in the local whiskey market in 2018. 'They came in a few years later than we did, and they developed the whiskey market. So that is one of the biggest challenges that we face now, but we have also added high-potential whisky products recently,' said Ei Phyo. One of the big international players, ThaiBev of Thailand, had also entered the Myanmar alcohol scene through a 75% stake in Grand Royal in 2017.

People Challenges

As the company grew, the founders took a more hands-off approach to managing the business. They became more involved at a strategic level, while the day-to-day running of the operations was left to senior management, which consisted of people who had been with the company for over 20 years, as well as recruits from the new generation.

However, with a large company of more than 1,000 people, a constant HR challenge was to find qualified middle management externally. Thus, PMG decided to groom its talent from within its ranks.

We know that middle managers, especially the talented ones, are quite rare and in extremely high demand. So, what we do is recruit either fresh graduates or people with about two years of work experience, and put them through our internal management training programme. The only requirement we have for them is to be smart and hardworking — the rest we can teach them. That is how we are growing the next generation of middle managers.

Besides looking within Myanmar for talent to hire, Tun Linn and Ei Phyo also travelled to job fairs in countries around the region that had Myanmar students graduating from university. They hoped that some of the Burmese citizens who studied in, for example, Singapore, Malaysia or Thailand, would be attracted by job offers from home.

New Product Lines for Myanmar People

As of 2018, PMG was a company with tens of millions of kyat in revenue. 'The future is exciting in the alcohol and water space,' said Ei Phyo.

The company was looking to carry out product innovations at affordable prices. 'I feel that Myanmar people have been exposed to a lot of cheap products. But just because a country is poor doesn't mean that it deserves cheap, low-quality products,' said Ei Phyo.

Traditionally, the alcohol market was segmented by price tiers. 'People would say "this is a 1,000-kyat, 2,000-kyat or 3,000-kyat bottle" and everything was price-driven,' she said. PMG recently made a bet by producing Freedom Whiskey, the first light whiskey in Myanmar, but at an existing price point. Ei Phyo explained, 'We want to innovate and let people try different things at the same price tier; expose them to international standards and flavours while not forgetting the inherent Myanmar characteristics.' The Freedom label alcohol was made from a blend of foreign imported liquor and Myanmar liquor. 'So that creates a unique flavour that you can't get even if you go to the United States. That's how we want to add value to the market.'

The *Crush!* product line represented another innovation, this time in bottled drinking water. While drinking water in Myanmar was typically packaged with sturdy and thick plastic bottles, *Crush!* was the first to be introduced with reduced plastic packaging. Ei Phyo hoped that this would be a means to educate people through the product,

> *Environment-friendly packaging is widely available internationally, but it hasn't been done in Myanmar yet. We want to use the opportunity to educate people to be more environmentally conscious. Everyone is going after the economic opportunities after the country started opening up, but we want to educate people on the environmental impact because we all share one world. So we're also trying to educate the public through our products. That's part of the vision of our company.*

Regrouping for the Future

Ei Phyo took stock of the avenues that the company might pursue in the future,

> *We don't have any plans to produce food, but because we have a manufacturing arm and also a distribution arm (Skyward), we can distribute beverages for both local or international companies that are looking to penetrate the Myanmar market.*

Assessing PMG's strengths in the market to date, she added,

> *Our rum portfolio is strong, and the whiskey part of our portfolio is being built up. There are already two or three very strong whiskey players in the market. Unless our product is different and is marketed differently, we're going to have to spend a lot of money going head-to-head with the market leaders. So we want to bring to market products that have something special about them.*

The domestic consumer's tastes are evolving, and so are the price points. But what was the outlook for internationalisation? PMG had previously explored exporting Myanmar Rum to China; however, the Chinese counterfeiters had immediately started creating knockoffs. Explained Ei Phyo,

> *In the medium-term, we want to produce more premium spirits locally and test it with the expatriates and tourists in Myanmar. They are a convenient test market for us. In that way, we can fine-tune the price point and the flavour profile. Once we have that set, then we will think about exporting to other countries, because we'll have a very specific marketing case for how we will penetrate other markets. Down the line that is something we are very interested in.*
>
> *As a 25-year-old company, we've not really taken stock of our heritage yet. We need a unique strategy or unique story to tell when we sell overseas, because people buy into the 'why' more so than the 'what'.*

Tun Linn encouraged entrepreneurs to look at venturing into the Myanmar market. He said,

> *Everyone has been saying it is the last frontier, but the point is there are actually a lot of difficulties in the market right now, and that's why this is the ideal time to come into the market. As a young entrepreneur, you will either make it and make a lot of money, or you won't, but the experience of operating through difficulties in a frontier market will be invaluable.*

Ei Phyo concluded,

> *The most satisfying part of running the business is bringing high-quality and safe products at affordable prices to*

people in a country that has been closed off. And the other part of it is that, for us, private sector work is a bit like community service. We develop people, not just products. Not only do we provide jobs to the local communities, we also invest in and groom our people, developing the next generation of leaders for Myanmar. Even if they leave the company later, they're going to do something great in other fields. I think that's how we're going to contribute to the country.

As Ei Phyo concluded, it was evident that the future of the Peace Myanmar Group was very bright. Solid sales, strong distribution and a history of innovation, experimentation and dealing with uncertainty were core strengths that had prepared them for Myanmar's next chapter. But don't expect them to read it, as they are actively trying to write it.

Chapter 6

YKKO: A FAMILY BUSINESS, A FAMILY RESTAURANT

Whenever you're doing something, you should put your heart into it and go the extra mile; not just to get your work done, but to do what is best. This is the philosophy behind the company.

— Aye Myat Maw, Director (Marketing and Business Development), YKKO

Yankin Kyay-oh, or YKKO, was a family restaurant that specialised in the Burmese noodle dish, kyay-oh. Starting off in 1988 as one small shop run from the family home in Yangon, by 2018 YKKO had transitioned to a second generation-run business that had expanded to 35 shops across five cities in Myanmar.

YKKO continued to operate as a predominantly family-owned business. However, as the firm grew, the family brought in local talent and professional management, which had enabled it to become a successful and efficient business. At its heart, however, the firm's DNA continued to strongly retain its motto of 'serving with our heart'.

Aye Myat Maw, Director (Marketing and Business Development), YKKO, explained how the company has grown from a small shop of four founders in Yangon in 1988, to a group with more than 1,500 employees spread across the larger cities of Myanmar.

Founded Amidst Unrest

YKKO started out at a difficult time in the Myanmar economy. In an incident known as the '8888 uprising', pro-democracy students had protested against the military government, leading to widespread riots and demonstrations across the nation. Against that backdrop of unrest, two young Burmese couples asked themselves, 'In this environment, what can we do to find work?'

This was the beginning of the story that Aye Myat recounted of how her parents and uncle and aunt opened the first YKKO store.

> *In 1988, a couple of months after the eighth of August revolutions, my mom and dad and my uncle and aunt, two young couples, thought about what to do for a living. They decided to use a small space in my grandparents' house (my father and my aunt's childhood home), which happened to be on the ground floor on Yankin Street, to start a store.*
>
> *At that time, my mother's side of the family used to live downtown on Shwe Taung Tan Street, which had a very famous and popular kyay-oh stall — Shwe Taung Tan Kyay-Oh. Kyay-oh was a Chinese soup dish traditionally made with vermicelli and pork.*

The couples had thought that as Yangon, and in particular Yankin Street, had a sizeable residential population, a store could do well. And kyay-oh was something that at that time was only found on the street sides off downtown Chinatown, so they decided to 'bring it to this residential area, make it more of a home-feel and improve it'. She added,

The name was very simple. We're selling kyay-oh in Yankin, so it was called Yankin Kyay-oh, referring to the original location of our very first stall in the Yankin district. Then it got abbreviated to YKKO when we expanded to more branches.

But, interestingly, neither couple knew how to cook the dish. They instead got the kyay-oh master from Shwe Taung Tan Kyay-Oh, who was, incidentally, quitting from his job at that time, to work at their new store.

Aye Myat's parents were involved in running the first two stores; from the third store onwards, they participated as investors. The operations, the main expansion and the heart of the company were run by Aye Myat's uncle, U Nyan Lin. He was the first Chairman of YKKO, and also the founder and first Chairman of the Myanmar Restaurant Association.

Kyay-oh was YKKO's signature dish. The shop started with some simple offerings on the menu: soup or dry, chicken or pork, and vermicelli or flat rice noodle. It was very much a customised dish for the individual.

It really took off on day one itself, and sales were good. It started off as a very small family unit. My parents were doing the serving. My uncle would wake up at 5 am to go to the wet market to buy ingredients. Sometimes my grandfather and mother would help with the accounts. And then, the cousins also came along and helped.

Five years later, in 1993, the family opened a second store on Saya San Road, another residential location not too far from the first store. Opportunity had knocked: 'My aunt and uncle were living in the area, and there was land available right beside their home,' said Aye Myat.

Because the first store was quite a success, some other family members and friends wanted to get involved. They chipped in mainly with their money and left the management to Aye Myat's uncle and aunt. 'My parents looked after the first store, and my aunt and uncle looked after the second store. That was when we took up the name YKKO, because we were no longer just in Yankin.'

Becoming More Popular

The new store struggled at first to keep afloat, but after about three years in 1996, it became a very popular hangout. Its décor, with a courtyard opening into a garden where people could sit outdoors, made it very attractive with the younger crowd. The store was also close to a family swimming pool, where many children would go to learn how to swim. Back then, there were only two or three swimming pools around Yangon, and families and couples would drop by YKKO on their way to or from the pool.

Over time, the menu expanded to the three basic pillars that are still found in all YKKO shops today — kyay-oh, grill and drinks counters. Aye Myat recalled,

> We added variations of Sichet, another type of dry-noodle dish, which could not be found elsewhere in the city (Yangon) besides the downtown area. We also added a grill counter for barbecue and satay, which was my uncle's mother's recipe. Our meat is slightly thinner because we want more marinade to go into the meat… The barbecue was also unique back then. You don't get this kind of marination elsewhere. After that, we added drinks.

The business remained as it was for the next 10 years, with just two stores doing well.

Expanding Through Franchising

In 2003, one of the existing business partners of YKKO expressed interest in starting a franchise to open new outlets. Aye Myat elaborated,

> *At that time, my aunt and uncle were also looking after other business ventures, and my mom and dad too were engaged in their own ventures. We were just happy to stay with the two stores.*
>
> *The partners got to know more about YKKO because my uncle had wanted to implement a more rigorous accounting system in the company. The partner and his wife, who is a qualified accountant, helped us with our accounts and got inspired by the business. They wanted to take out a franchise, and my uncle suggested, "Okay, why don't we form a partnership?"*

That year, the third YKKO store opened under its first partnership arrangement. It also marked the introduction of financial and management control systems into the company. In retrospect, this was an essential step in preparing the firm for the future growth it would experience. Rigorous accounting, reporting and transparency made it easier to diagnose problems, correct shortcomings, assure investors and attract funds.

The year 2005 saw the opening of the fourth store, and in 2007, the first store outside Yangon was opened in Nay Pyi Taw, the country's new administrative capital. Aye Myat said,

At the time, Nay Pyi Taw was still developing. There weren't many restaurants available. My mom was a civil servant, and she had to go there for work. She saw the potential for opening a branch there and talked to my uncle, who also saw the potential because there wasn't much competition back then. If you are the first mover, you have the advantage. You have a ready-made market.

By 2010, YKKO had opened 11 stores. From the fourth to the 11th outlet, stores were individually managed by different partners. Existing partners had the option of investing in the next new outlet if they wanted to. Each outlet then had a different shareholding allocation and management team. 'Stores numbers four to 11 were not really franchisees because the family was also investing. It was about getting new people who could look after the new stores,' said Aye Myat.

For YKKO, a bottleneck to growth was the managerial capacity needed beyond the initial founders. Thus, the new investors were not just capital investors, but also required to be a part of operations to ensure the success of the new restaurant. However, with the addition of new partners, subsequent cross-ownerships were becoming very confusing. 'Every store had a different manager and different investors. It was a huge task to work these out accounting-wise.'

Things came to a head in 2010. The solution was a consolidation of all the shareholdings.

The shareholders trusted Aye Myat's uncle to reapportion the overall shareholdings of all the outlets to each individual shareholder, depending on how much money each had contributed earlier.

Apart from the first two stores, we put the rest of the stores into a company. We had to do a bit of bookkeeping and negotiations and agreements… It was not challenging because a lot of the partners who had been involved since the third store were still partners. What my uncle did was to not only consolidate the company, but also manage the shareholding regarding how much each shareholder could contribute back to the company. When he said, 'Okay, you cannot contribute much to the company in terms of your time, so don't take such a large shareholding; you just take this percentage, and the rest you take in cash,' people would listen.

Forming a Company

In 2011, YKKO was incorporated as a corporate entity. The new entities soon realised economies of scale as departments such as HR, procurement and operations were centralised rather than separately managed by each outlet and their specific holdings. 'It was a much cleaner way to manage the business,' said Aye Myat.

Centralising functions under one corporate entity also helped solving other issues. Besides resolving accounting challenges and shareholder allocations, costs were better managed and the consistency of brand image was maintained. Training, advertising, work rules, payments, billings, receivables, career management and employee turnover became centrally controlled, and accordingly prioritised and consistent across the firm.

Aye Myat commented, 'Previously, whenever a new store opened, it was a case of "Okay, who will take more shares? Who will take fewer shares?" But with the consolidation, we managed to solve these problems and gain economies of scale.' The resulting consistency of quality in the stores and front-of-house image also helped to strengthen YKKO's brand identity as the consistency of look, feel and experience was evident.

In addition, the formation of YKKO as a corporate entity allowed the company to expand in a coordinated, and yet aggressive, manner. 'We wanted to expand more, but having one shareholder assigned to one store became quite a limiting factor. That was the management potential of forming a head office; it just made sense.'

In 2012, the year Aye Myat came back from her studies at Cambridge University in the UK, the company had a total of 16 stores, and by 2014, that had more than doubled to 34 stores. In 2015, YKKO boasted 37 stores across five cities in Myanmar — Yangon, Mandalay, Nay Pyi Taw, Bago and Mawlamyaing.

The period 2016–2018 saw YKKO taking a closer look at its existing portfolio, identifying under-performing assets and closing them, while also opening new branches in new locations with greater potential. As of 2018, YKKO had 35 outlets.

Managing Challenges

Building Management Capabilities

In 2018, YKKO was looking to make a transition to the next level. In order to do that, there were several everyday realities of doing business that had to be managed. Aye Myat explained,

> It makes a lot of sense at some point to take a look and see what's doing well, and what's not. Obviously, what we were doing was moving very much away from a mom-and-pop-oriented family business towards centralised management, management systems and professional management.

In terms of building management capabilities, finding the supply of appropriately skilled human capital across all levels was the biggest challenge. Myanmar had not had a long history of professionally run organisations, and finding middle and senior managers that had experience overseeing 20 or more employees was hard to find. Aye Myat elaborated,

> *Human capital is particularly challenging, and at each level it's difficult. At the entry level, frontline staff need a lot of training. Also, the education level among the staff is very different. We have to train them on not only how to serve the customer, but also how they should portray themselves, how they should smile, what level of personal hygiene they need to maintain, what is acceptable and what is not. That kind of training takes time. The past five to six years have been difficult in this area, especially the last three years, when F&B has boomed.*
>
> *Since the country opened up after 2011, many foreign brands came in and many people started new restaurants, thinking that it's a relatively easy business to enter. That demand for human capital has been challenging, particularly at the middle level, where people keep poaching our managers. We are the easiest target to obtain locals with the right skillsets.*
>
> *At the senior level, it's also challenging because we've never had such skills in this country, where senior managers have had to manage ten plus stores. I think even today, it's very difficult to find people who can manage 20, 30 stores. And if you do find them, there will be somebody else who is looking for them as well. It's the kind of talent that's in short supply and high demand.*

But there were also many other challenges at the time. Other than the daily question of offering political and civil stability in Myanmar as a conducive climate for business and foreign investors, there was also the question of affordability of products in different regions. Aye Myat added,

> When we wanted to expand, we tested our product in three other cities apart from the current five cities that we're in, and we found that regional spending power is quite low. People will be very excited when we go to their towns, and they'll come to us for the first six months, and we'll see really good sales. But then, later on, they will go back to eating at home or at their local stores, which are much cheaper, because, of course, they don't have the costs we do in terms of the whole setup. The regional spending power is still not there.

Rental increases were also an area of rising costs. While YKKO's first few stores were all standalone, the company gradually started opening its new outlets in shopping malls, where there was higher footfall. While the strategy to use the location to attract more customers was successful, the rental fees had not been kind on the margins. 'A lot of the newer malls are asking for really outrageous rentals. The property price and rent costs just keeps on going up,' said Aye Myat.

As business improved and the company expanded, it ran into the problem of procurement — obtaining an adequate supply of ingredients for dishes, as well as logistic challenges in getting supply to the right locations at the right time in the right quantity. Aye Myat said,

> The biggest challenge that we had three to four years back was getting enough supply for our store consumption because we were selling well, but our suppliers had a limit to what they could supply us. Or they could supply us, but

they couldn't transport to all our stores. We had to invest a lot more in our own logistic fleet to cover the last mile.

The biggest challenge for the company, though, was yet to come.

Change is Inevitable

In 2015, Aye Myat's uncle, Lin, passed away unexpectedly. Although it did not take the family entirely by surprise as he had been having health issues, it was difficult for anyone to step in and fill his shoes. In time, Daw Yu Yu Lwin, his wife and co-founder, took over YKKO as Chairman.

Lin had been very clearly the leader in the company, and he embodied the values of the company — everyone, family members and investors alike, turned to him for advice and the final say on matters. Added Aye Myat,

His vision was that YKKO should be a Myanmar brand that everybody looks up to and also one that lasts for centuries.

He was always driven to be the first mover in the F&B industry, to provide quality products in Myanmar. He lived and breathed the company motto "Serving with our hearts"... Ever since we started from store number one, we only served people what we would serve our own family, because family meals have always been very important to us, and to our culture as well. He would say that every customer is actually not a customer, but a guest. You wouldn't serve your guest what you wouldn't eat. You have to serve with your heart. This applies across all levels of the company in terms of food, service staff, as well as head office staff.

Although many new food concepts were entering the market, such as pop-up stalls that had become a very popular sight, Aye Myat was confident that people would keep coming back to YKKO for the food, as well as the place, and the atmosphere.

Maintaining a Consistent Brand Image

At the end of the day, what kept Aye Myat up at night was ensuring the delivery of quality and consistency across all products across each of the stores.

Bringing up the human capital challenge once again, she commented,

> The staff at the frontline need to be well-trained. They're relatively young in the company, yet they are the ones who are actually meeting the customers. The customers see YKKO through them. It's really not easy when there is a lot of turnover. That is something that our HR team will have to work very hard on. Brands are built on consistency and the ability to deliver on their promise. These front-line staff are critical in this effort.

In April 2017, YKKO set up a central kitchen. It was a huge investment, aimed at scaling up its food processing as well as controlling costs. Earlier in 2014, the company had set up a central warehouse to store its inventory and distribute it to its outlets. It also used to have five big kitchens in its larger restaurants, to prepare and stock different semi-prepared ingredients that the stores in the shopping malls needed (as shopping malls could not have a large kitchen space, some preprocessing of the food was useful). Aye Myat explained,

> Moving to a central kitchen involved shifting from a relatively smaller scale to a larger one and there were other

costs involved. But we needed to take that step because otherwise we cannot control quality and food safety in the way we want to. Centralising led to an opportunity to limit variations and provide consistency. We want every bowl of kyay-oh to be of a good standard. We don't want that to change. When you have a brand, it has to be managed in the marketplace. Trying to run 11 restaurants with 11 different ownership structures and 11 different managers — and maybe making their own special broth with local adaptations — you become very vulnerable to some sort of quality issue in one of the restaurants.

This step in the journey of YKKO is often encountered in the entrepreneurial journey to scale up. That is, it isn't until you begin to plan the dream and understand where you are going that you realise the need for this. Day-to-day steps are often based on what makes sense for the location. But at times you need to step back and ask, 'What is the right way to do things if you are going to expand?' It's not just about whether we get the right things for our stores, or whether we get fresh ingredients. Essentially, our final delivery has to be tasty. It's something that we have always stood for. We don't want that to change.

Where To Go From Here?

Aye Myat added,

It's the culture that makes this place different, the kind of place that people want to work in, or a place that customers want to come to. Essentially, it's about serving with our heart. We've brought kyay-oh to a lot of locations across Yangon, so it has become very convenient for people to go to. It's a comfortable place for you to sit, or in some of the biggest stores, to even work, for a while. Smaller stores always promise a comfort meal, where you know what *you're going to get. It's not something new. It has always been there, and it will be there for you.*

What's in store for the future? YKKO was looking into extending the range of food concepts that it offered. Previously, it had tested the idea of barbecue Korean chicken, something which did not manage to take off after three years. It was now looking at introducing boat noodles, a Thai soupy noodle dish. Aye Myat concluded,

For YKKO to continue to expand, we will need to go to a more lower-priced segment than what we are currently targeting, making kyay-oh more affordable so that it can cater to more regions than the major cities that we are reaching at the moment... Eventually, we want to be a Myanmar brand that the people all around the region will recognise. To do that, we will need to step out of the country.

Chapter 7

BEAUTY PALACE: THE CHANGE ADVOCATE

I am Burmese and proud to be one. I would like to serve my country and my people in any way I can. I've been given this chance to witness and be part of the transition of one of the world's fastest growing economies. I could not be in a better place than where I am right now. I am glad to be part of history as a change advocate, and want to do things differently.

— Chua Meimei, Board Director of United Beauty Palace Myanmar

In her mid-twenties, Chua Meimei returned to Burma to helm her father's personal care business, Beauty Palace. With just one year of outside work experience under her belt, but a lifetime of hands-on learning about her family business and its intricacies, the spunky Singapore Management University business graduate had to stand up to change-resistant management and forge a new path for the company. Under her lead, the company would enter into a joint venture with the Philippines' largest pharmaceutical company United Laboratories, Inc., to establish United Beauty Palace, the second largest personal care company in Myanmar.

For Meimei, it has been a long, tough battle. But she does not plan to rest until she reaches her goal: to turn her home-grown brands into international brands and establish a foothold for United Beauty Palace in the global market.

A Story that Began with a Sour Note

Beauty Palace started in 2000 as a partnership among four men: three men related by blood and Myaing Hin, Meimei's father. In those days, Beauty Palace's chief product was a beauty soap that was a Burmese equivalent to Lux. Things, however, eventually soured among the partners.

Besides Beauty Palace, the four men co-founded other startups. Time and again, as each of the startups became profitable, Myaing Hin would be cut from the money-maker. Finally, Myaing Hin decided that he had had enough. The partnership was dissolved in 2004 and in the ensuing bidding battle, Myaing Hin successfully outbid his three former partners to gain sole control of the firm. However, despite the victory, the price he paid for the firm was high.

Recounted Meimei, 'The three partners thought my dad was silly to bid so much for the brand when they had the knowhow and could easily set up the business again.'

The partners did just that. They set up a company to sell a rival beauty soap that was a duplicate of Beauty Palace's soap. What was more, they contracted Beauty Palace's distributor, Pioneer Group, to distribute their soap on an exclusive basis, cutting Beauty Palace out of the action.

Instead of deterring Myaing Hin, this made him even more determined to make a success of Beauty Palace. Meimei recounted her father's actions,

He asked his staff to park a minivan outside the office of Pioneer Group at the end of the company's workday. He waited at the gate and as the employees of Pioneer Group were walking out, he announced, "Whoever wants to join Beauty Palace, get on the bus." Half of the team from Pioneer Group got on the bus. It was at that moment that Beauty Palace's internal distribution arm was born.

I have to thank the former partners for that. Without distribution, we would be just a manufacturing facility and could never have done better than the companies that were ahead of us in terms of technological knowhow. The local insights we derive from our distribution operation give us a vital edge and make us a cut above everyone else. And it is this distribution strength that is keeping us in the market at this point in time.

Beauty Palace went on to launch Best-T, which grew to be the market-leading gel toothpaste in Myanmar, surpassing brands from giants such as Colgate and Unilever. The company also launched a shampoo and Pro-Care, an anti-bacterial soap, and numerous other products.

Meanwhile, the company set up by the three former partners folded in 2010. This was a time that witnessed great consolidation in the personal care market in Myanmar as raw material prices for soap manufacturing shot up. This input-based cost escalation squeezed many players. With counterfeit products available, and porous borders that allowed manufacturers from neighbouring countries with greater scale and access to capital to enter via grey markets, the Myanmar market was a hard place to pass on such cost increases.

Undergoing Executive Training Since 10 Years of Age

In 2008, Meimei, who was previously working in Singapore, returned to Myanmar to help her father manage Beauty Palace.

But could a business graduate with just one year of formal work experience lead a firm? The truth was that Meimei had been undergoing business management training since she was 10 years old.

While she was enrolled in a primary school in Singapore, her father opened a bank account in Singapore. With no trusted staff on the island, he co-opted Meimei to handle his business transactions there, including running his bank facilities and authorising bank transfers. She learned to fill up Telegraphic Transfer (TT) forms carefully, as her father did not condone mistakes. She said,

> *I was only in Primary four and I had to go to the banks to execute TT transfers. I had to go to the shipping lines to reconcile shipments and help switch bills of landing. I went to all the ministries to hand in applications. Every day, after school, while my friends headed out to play, I had to call my dad and ask him: "Are there any TTs for me?"*

Every school holiday, she returned to Myanmar where she was put to work at the office. Her father also brought Meimei along on his business meetings in the region because he spoke very little English. He would explain to Meimei the business context of each meeting so that she would be able to translate the discussions. At these meetings, she learnt first-hand the art of negotiation. 'When it comes to business, I was definitely far ahead of my peers. At a young age, I had already acquired that gut feel which usually comes from experience,' she said.

Captain of a Mutinous Crew

To the management team of Beauty Palace, however, Meimei was a young, inexperienced brash upstart who did not know her place. That led to numerous boardroom clashes.

By the time she joined Beauty Palace, the company had already gone through three different management teams because of the challenges of managing the organisation.

One was that the management ranks were packed with family members. A cousin was Myaing Hin's right-hand man, while his long serving executive assistant was another key man, making human resource management a daunting affair.

Steering Beauty Palace was also tricky because all the managers held information close to their chest. The warehouse director, for instance, would not reveal how much stock he had. Meimei commented,

> I couldn't plan because everyone was secretive. It was very hard for me to access information and to learn. In the first two years back in Myanmar, I cried more than I cried in my entire 25 years combined. And I am not a person who cries easily. What made it worse was that I came back for my dad, but he wasn't really on my side.

The infighting exploded into open warfare in November 2009, when Meimei went head-on with the intractable management. Offended at being questioned by Meimei, 10 of the 11 department heads handed in their resignations on the same day. Myaing Hin's response was to command his daughter to apologise and coax the resignees back to work. However, Meimei refused.

> I told him, "If I am not able to contribute, why am I leading the company? If I was to lead the company, there had to be changes and it had to be my style, my way."

Myaing Hin gave his daughter two weeks to get a new team and have the operations up and running again. Pull that off and she would have free rein in running Beauty Palace. Fail and she would have to apologise to the managers and get them back. Meimei shot back: 'Ok. Deal!'

For the first 12 days, Meimei camped out in the HR department to understand the organisation and its operational needs. On the last two days, she went on a hiring frenzy. With jobs scarce in Myanmar, she managed to assemble a good team. As of 2018, almost all of her hires remained part of the management team.

The Change Advocate

As Managing Director of Beauty Palace, Meimei proceeded to revolutionise the organisation.

She recruited more female employees, removed gender-specific roles and more than halved the average age of employees from 53 to the early 20s. She explained,

> We needed to be fast, and we needed to be dynamic. This was because we were lagging behind the competition. We were not number one in the market. So, there was a lot of catching up to do. We could not afford to go leisurely at our pace. We had to run three times faster if we wanted to be ahead of our competitors. Even before the opening up of Myanmar, we had to move fast. This was the mentality that I adopted. It wasn't easy for the team, but they did change for which I am very thankful.

In the decade that followed, Meimei incessantly turned the company around. Wearing the hat of a change advocate, Meimei spent about two hours each day with a small group of employees to talk about the direction the company is charting. She said,

The company is subjected to change, change, change, change, change all the time. Change has been the new normal for my team. If they are not being directed to change, they would wonder, "Am I being left out? Have I been forgotten?" Change has become part of our culture. In short, I created a team that believes in change.

Leading from the Front

From the start, Meimei was right out there in the frontline along with her distribution team.

For instance, piqued by the market potential of Tan Yan town in the Shan State, she decided to visit the town, unaware that it was a 'grey' area rife with ethnic armed groups. The journey took the team deep into the jungle, where there were no roads. Meimei constantly discerned movement out of the corner of her eyes. She spotted children with guns and naively asked if the guns were for hunting. 'I didn't know that all the time we were on that trek, there was someone shadowing us, either the military or the ethnic armed groups,' she recounted.

On another market research trip, she stayed at a hotel located next to the police station, not knowing that just a week before, the police station had been bombed by an armed ethnic group. She said,

It never occurred to me that it was dangerous. I just knew that I needed to go to the market in order to be where the consumer is and to understand what her needs are. I also wanted to show the team that I will go wherever they go. I needed to let them know that if I ask them to go to an area, it has to be an area that I dare to go myself. Another

> *reason is that it gives me a chance to understand my team and them to know me better. So, we continued building a relationship at the ground level.*

Secret to Success: A Highly Efficient Distribution Network

Without a technical team, the chief strength of Beauty Palace was its distribution prowess. For this reason, from the very beginning, Meimei focused on building up her distribution network.

For greater control and deeper penetration, Beauty Palace distributed directly to its retail customers, rather than relying solely on third-party sub-distributors for last-mile distribution.

As of 2018, the company distributed to eight key provinces and maintained eight depots, significantly fewer than competitors that had 12 to 20 depots. Despite this, the distribution network of Beauty Palace was exceptionally efficient. Though Beauty Palace offered far fewer products than its competitors, the company generated a higher average revenue per invoice, enhancing the cost efficiency. She said,

> *I have been crunching a lot of numbers and the comparisons showed we were — and still are — very efficient in distribution, compared to our competitors. That is because we are using what we have, like our local knowledge, to our advantage.*

Caring Mother Figure, Wily HR Manager

Meimei added, 'You really have to think of very creative ways of managing HR.'

Beauty Palace's distribution strength derived from its team of loyal and dynamic distribution managers. This team had been carefully groomed by Meimei, who had to continually contend with the possibility of embezzlement; it was very easy for an employee with access to the company's money and stock to abscond with both and scoot across the Thai border until it was safe for him/her to return to Myanmar. Meimei knew she needed to reduce this risk. 'Should someone abscond, I would lose a potential sales talent in whom I have invested so much,' she said.

Meimei used a fascinating stratagem to mitigate this risk — by playing a mother figure and HR maven. She also always promoted a sense of family within the firm. 'How far can you run with a wife and kids?' she said with a smile.

To achieve that, she would stage and manage the most intimate facets of her managers' lives in a way that would advance their careers and financial well-being while securing their service to the company.

Her strategy derived from an understanding of the Burmese psyche. The Myanmar people had gone through endless rounds of political upheavals and sea changes through the decades. That bitter experience had taught them not to plan for the future. What is the use, they thought, when some event will come along to disrupt their plans? As a counterpoise, Meimei took on the job of life planner for her staff. She explained,

> They do not have an idea of how to plan their life, and so,
> I break down their goals for them. I get to know each and
> every one of them. Then I start to encourage them to have
> girlfriends. After they date for a while, I would tell them that

now is the time to get married. After they get married, I would send them to the branches. At that point, I would tell them that now that you are married, it's time you have kids. With the wedding, their savings is depleted. So, I would also tell them, you have to start saving for your kids' education. All this gives them something to work towards in their personal life.

Meimei's stratagem had proven to be effective. While competitors have had to shut down operations because their staff ran away with stock and money, Beauty Palace has not experienced a single case of embezzlement since Meimei headed the firm.

The case of the Love-Struck Sales Supervisor

There was a sales supervisor who had been courting his girlfriend for more than a decade. Their relationship, however, was impeded because of objections from the girl's parents. Meimei recalled,

One day I asked him: "Let's say you wait another 10 years, will anything change?" He said no. I told him, "I don't understand what you are waiting for. Are you waiting for a miracle to happen?" I left the conversation at that.

Next morning, he came to me and said: "I am going to elope with my girlfriend tonight. So, I am going to take leave for the next three days." I told him, "Great! If there's anything you need, let me know."

When the couple eloped, Meimei posted the supervisor to a branch to provide the newly weds with company housing (and a bit of distance from his in-laws) and gave the new bride a position in Beauty Palace to supplement the couple's income.

The move was also a great HR ploy for Beauty Palace. In the early years, Beauty Palace employees were dead set against moving to a branch office, preferring to be close to their families. With no employee willing to move out of Yangon, it was hard for Beauty Palace to grow in some of the emerging up-country markets. Meimei needed to change that mindset and the sales supervisor was the perfect candidate for that. When the company eventually posted the supervisor back to Yangon, Beauty Palace loaned him the money to buy a house.

Not forgotten or banished by the company, but rather brought back and extended a home loan, the employee was an example of how loyalty was a two-way street. In 2018, that same supervisor was the head of Beauty Palace's biggest branch office in Yangon, where he was leading sales growth in the high double-digits for the firm.

Companies in Myanmar may be suffering from rampant poaching of their talents, but Meimei was proud to declare that she had zero turnover among her valued distribution team. 'It is only because of their support it is possible for the company to be where it is today,' she said.

Playing in the Big League

When she first returned to Myanmar, Meimei wondered if her generation would ever see Myanmar open its market.

Nevertheless, she began to prepare for that day. She knew Beauty Palace had to evolve as a company to face the onslaught of global players once the market opened up. Her plan was to form a joint venture to acquire the competitive strength needed to fend off the giants. She said,

The company has a lot of potential and it would be such a waste to have its growth limited by the person fronting the

company, which is me. I am still learning on the job and there are so many limitations to what I can do, and expertise that I do not have.

In 2011, while she was still surveying potential joint venture partners, the market sprung open. The turn of events meant that her plans had to be sped up. But first she had to convince her conservative father. She explained,

Partnering with a total stranger that is a foreign company to boot wasn't an easy choice for my dad. I told him this is the way to stay ahead of the competition unless we have very deep pockets to fight against Procter & Gamble, Unilever and all these MNCs.

In the end, Myaing Hin agreed to enter a joint venture. After exploring several candidates, Beauty Palace chose to partner with United Laboratories, Inc., (Unilab), the Philippines' pharmaceutical giant. In 2015, Beauty Palace and Unilab came together to form United Beauty Palace Myanmar Co., Ltd., with Meimei fronting the joint venture as its managing director. The collaboration has seen a union of strengths: Unilab has brought technology and knowhow to the table, while Beauty Palace contributed local insights. Meimei said,

Today [2018] we still look like an SME, but we have a US$1 billion company and over 3,000 staff behind us. And that changes things. Take global sourcing. We now have a dedicated team of 60 people from Unilab helping us do global sourcing. So, things get done very fast.

The company is bracing for a brutal showdown ahead. She added,

Colgate-Palmolive has entered the market. And recently Unilever just bought over Europe and Asia Commercial, the

largest player in Myanmar's personal care market. This means that Unilever now has production facilities. Unilever already has the money, global supply chains, and the muscle, and now it is building up new ammunition.

Meimei reckoned Beauty Palace would have been pushed out of the market in just three years if it had remained on its own. But she believes that the combined strengths of Unilab and Beauty Palace would serve United Beauty Palace well in the upcoming battle. She said,

I think we have the edge over Unilever and Colgate-Palmolive being local because the terrains are tough and we know them well. Even now, when we are in the middle of a civil war, our sales don't drop. There may be a war going on, but our products reach consumers. Unlike us, Unilever will never send its staff to troubled parts of Myanmar. But we know the safe window to move goods through — which is when the rebels rest — and we get it done during this period.

It was going to be a long, draining, tough fight. 'We just have to up our game. It's no longer competition within the local league anymore. Now we are competing in the champion's league', Meimei concluded.

Section 3

TECHNOLOGY

Myanmar's recent social and political reforms signal a move forward on the path to transforming and reintegrating into the world economy. To do so, the technical sector will need to develop rapidly. In a society with limited public resources and low digital literacy rates, entrepreneurs have been, and will be, an essential partner in the journey. In this book, we had an opportunity to meet and interview some of the most successful, creative and out-of-the-box thinkers.

As we began investigating the entrepreneurial scene in Myanmar, we were pointed in the direction of Yangon's Phandeeyar. Self-described as 'an innovation lab that is spearheading the use of technology to accelerate change and development in Myanmar,'[1] Phandeeyar was a beehive of activity, where we watched and met young would-be entrepreneurs combining dreams, ingenuity, passion and technology into business plans. It became very evident, very quickly, that this would be the kind of raw resources that would lead Myanmar into the next decade and beyond. Whether it was incubation activities, office spacing, skill development, hackathons

---

[1] Phandeeyar company website, https://www.phandeeyar.institute/.

and gamification competitions, or business plan assistance and funding, Phandeeyar and several of the entrepreneurs whom we will feature in this section of the book were there, spurring on this nascent sector.

Today, there are several innovation labs and incubators sprouting in Yangon and Mandalay. The role they provide as a talent magnate is, in and of itself, a crucial step in marshalling, organising and deploying technology resources in a society such as Myanmar. Serving the role as connector, consolidator and igniter, these centres are bringing talent to the markets that are deploying technology.

The first time we visited Phandeeyar, it was at the request of Wai Phyo Kyaw, COO and co-founder of CarsDB.com, an avid technologist. Observing his rapport with the aspiring entrepreneurs, it was easy to see how a company such as CarsDB had been able to go beyond a simple ecommerce site to introducing buyers and sellers looking to acquire or dispose of automotives. CarsDB has organised the official automobile body of Myanmar. Leapfrogging the traditional physical showroom and service-bay model, Wai Phyo and the CarsDB team have been able to do this in a digital world, creating a platform for all things automotive. From three friends studying abroad, debating if they should return home, today the group boasts of three million impressions a month from more than 300,000 unique visitors, and more than 10,000 automotives available for sale at any time. Connecting buyers and sellers was just a start for a company that now also links the automobile owner to after-purchase service shops, detailers and accessories. CarsDB has had an incredible journey, considering that in 2013, Myanmar had an estimated 409,000 registered automobiles.[2]

---

[2] Molly Moore, Statista.com, 'Number of registered passenger cars in Myanmar from 2013 to 2019', 4 September 2020.

As Myanmar develops, the challenges of being globally competitive and digitally transforming will need to be balanced. At the tip of the spear is Nexlabs, a company that is working with Myanmar businesses to digitally transform their processes. Founder Ye Myat Min takes us on a journey of ups and downs, experiments and learnings, as he came upon the 'true business model' of his firm — reducing pain points.

In Flymya, we see Mike Than Tun Win, Flymya's CEO and founder, establish a company that has provided new opportunities for mom-and-pop retailers, consumers and tourists alike. Originally a site for travel, Flymya has migrated into solving the problems associated with payment methods and enabling local merchants and their neighbourhood customers the same access and purchasing experience that online customers enjoy. Flymya is one of the fastest growing enterprises in Southeast Asia, and is beginning to expand its reach beyond Myanmar's borders.

Completing our tech sector is Blue Ocean Operating Management, or BOOM for short. BOOM is a group of seven subsidiaries run by CEO Htun Htun Naing (commonly known as Nelson). A serial entrepreneur, Nelson has been involved in SIM card distribution, information assistance, staffing and business process outsourcing. But within his series of companies, he is investing in the next generation of Myanmar, and in a large part, the technology sector. It was with the goal of helping budding Burmese entrepreneurs that Nelson founded the Myanmar Young Entrepreneurs' Association in 2012. It started with less than 200 members, and by 2018, that number has grown to about 1,800.

Myanmar will probably not be viewed as a technology leader anytime soon. However, the creativity and passion of the entrepreneurs we met points to a bright future as technology adopters and practitioners.

Chapter 8

CarsDB — ROLLING WITH THE CHANGING MYANMAR ECONOMY

We are the go-to place for car enthusiasts in Myanmar. Our mission is to provide one-stop info on cars and related accessories and services. We want to make it easy for buyers and sellers to find one another on a platform that is efficient, quick and transparent.

— Wai Phyo Kyaw, COO, CarsDB

CarsDB is a quintessential example of business model innovation. The firm has constantly adapted to market and local government changes to fill the emerging demand for automobiles, car parts and accessories, after-sales servicing and resale. What was started by three close friends as a technical play to introduce buyers and sellers in a market (Myanmar) with limited buying patterns and consumer experience has now branched out to be a comprehensive site for all car-related matters for everyone, from the novice to mechanics, to even the experienced collector. Along the way, the offerings, customer-focus and revenue models have had to change to meet the burgeoning demands.

From its beginnings in 2012 as a used-car resale platform connecting buyers and sellers, CarsDB has grown to a well-known online new and used car and car accessories, parts and services sales platform in Myanmar, which by 2018 was receiving 10 million views from 300,000 unique users a month. Despite the speed and size of its growth, the company was careful to maintain its strong identity and values as a startup with integrity.

A business with its wheels turning smoothly, run by three friends who knew one another like family, it boasted about 50 employees by 2018. Wai Phyo Kyaw, COO, saw the business as a confluence of technology, advertising and e-commerce.

Starting with What You Know to Enter New Avenues of Potential

From a young age of 15, Wai Phyo, who was listed in 2017 Forbes Magazine 30 Under 30 Entrepreneurs in Myanmar, had been interested in software engineering and technology. It was not a leap of imagination in terms of taking an educational opportunity to move to Singapore in 2005, where he studied IT at Singapore Polytechnic. There he met two people who subsequently became his two co-founders for CarsDB — Wai Yan Lin, who became the CEO, and Myat Min Han, the future CTO. In 2011, he graduated with a degree in Information Systems from Singapore Management University.

Around the time of his graduation from university, Wai Yan made a trip to Myanmar and saw an opportunity in the used car market. He explained, 'It was the end of 2011, and the government had already opened up the domestic market, allowing anybody to import cars. Before that, it was totally locked down — nobody could import cars without a valid permit, which cost tens of thousands of dollars,' he said. Imports of Japanese automobiles surged in Myanmar after the deregulation of used-car imports in 2012.[3]

> *A lot of people started contacting overseas car dealers, typically based in Japan or Europe, and started importing units from these markets. This was especially true for Japan, which had always wanted to export their used inventory of rentals. Myanmar and other emerging markets love to buy from them.*

At the end of 2011, Wai Phyo and his co-founders completed the prototype for a website, which enabled people to list, then buy and sell used cars in Myanmar. A home-grown website created by three former roommates who had studied and lived together abroad, CarsDB was officially launched on 4 January 2012, to coincide with Myanmar's Independence Day.

Addressing a Gaping Need in the Industry

CarsDB was created to solve the challenge of matching the gap between buyers and sellers in the automobile market. Before Wai Phyo and his team created the platform, people just bought and sold cars in the physical marketplace. Commented Wai Phyo,

> *If you wanted to sell a used car, you had to drive your car to a big physical lot or an open space to meet the brokers and car buyers. The buyers, too, would have to physically come down and look at the cars. So you have to travel, and you waste your time and energy. You don't know what you're getting beforehand. The prices are not transparent at all.*

---

[3] Motokazu Matsui and Takemi Nakagawa, 'Myanmar's Car Market Set to take New Direction', *Financial Times*, 2 January 2017.

People just quoted as much as they like. So it was a very difficult, very opaque market.

So we told everybody not to waste their energy and resources this way, and began providing them with an online marketplace where anybody who wanted a car could just purchase it on our platform. Buyers can connect to sellers by calling them directly, emailing or messaging them, and carry out the transaction at a convenient location. It was a simple classified advertising model, which was not very popular in Myanmar at that time.

After CarsDB was officially launched in January 2012, traction for the site came naturally. Early on this meant mostly Yangon, which was the port where the car imports would arrive. 'People were excited about looking for cars to buy because the government had liberalised imports. So let's say for a 2007 Toyota Camry, which would've cost you hundreds of thousands of dollars prior to 2011, it would only cost you about $40,000 in 2012,' he said.

CarsDB also provided verified information, such as mileage and accident history of the car, for buyers to compare with other vehicles.

After six months, the website was acquiring 20–30 car listings — but by the end of 2012, it was adding cars for sale at a rate of 7,000 cars a year. Despite such an impressive run rate, the site was not becoming a huge cash churning machine. It only started to make money when it adjusted its listing fee policies and expanded its scope of services.

Going Local

CarsDB's strategy was to first increase the volume of content, particularly about cars, on the website. It ran on a classifieds model, to gain critical mass and become viable in the long-term on the supply side. It targeted parties with a large inventory, which were usually businesses rather than individuals. Up until mid-2012, the platform was largely used by foreign importers.

Then, Wai Phyo and his team started talking to the local car dealers to list their inventory on CarsDB. It was a process of having to educate each broker and dealer about the business one by one, to get him or her to adopt the site. 'These guys knew everything about cars, inside and out. But they had no clue about technology. For those that didn't want to use the site, we had to gain their trust by demonstrating value,' he said. It helped that Yangon was then undergoing a real estate boom, and renting showroom space was expensive compared to selling cars online. The team also had to educate the importers, acquiring them one by one. It took a while before the team signed up their first 10,000 users.

The Website: A Growing Business that Adapts and Evolves

The website started off with a simple model. It was a freemium model, where any buyer or seller could sign up for free, and add on premium (paid) options (such as a more prominent product listing for a potentially faster sale). Later on, a listing fee of US$10 a week was introduced. CarsDB also subsequently added features such as car seller rankings and visibility settings to fine-tune the service offering further, and make the website more useful and powerful for the consumer, while beginning to establish criteria for evaluating sellers to encourage reputable behaviour in a developing market.

The content and contacts that were obtained from the site would belong to the dealers, which incentivised them to use the site and also provide content to improve the site. This alignment of the site's policy to the dealer's goals was a major step in gaining commitment, continuity and trust. But, as mentioned before, the early pricing model did not create an enormous cash engine.

Committing to the Business

At the end of 2012, Wai Phyo and his team decided that it was time to leave their jobs in Singapore.

> *At the time, we were already pretty settled down in our jobs in Singapore, having been there for more than seven years. We also had family and friends there. But the three of us decided to return to Myanmar and get more involved in the business.*

The decision to move paid off handsomely. By the end of 2013, CarsDB had nearly tripled its number of listings to about 20,000 cars.

Raising Funds

CarsDB had been incorporated in Singapore, with a fully-owned subsidiary operating in Myanmar. Raising funds for the business in Singapore was not easy because people did not know much about Myanmar and were hesitant to invest in the country. Prior to The Myanmar Citizens Investment Law of 2013, raising money abroad was quite difficult (not that it became much easier quickly).

When the team was still based in Singapore, they were in bootstrapping mode — ploughing whatever the business had earned back into developing the website and paying a small team of part-time professionals. But committing to growth was also about expanding the team. In order to do that, the company had to raise funds.

In late 2013, CarsDB finally obtained its first round of angel investing. That only happened when it had hit a threshold of 15,000 listings — when the business looked viable and sustainable enough — convincing investors to put their first dollar into the business. Wai Phyo said,

> *In 2013, we were lucky to find an angel investor. Trying to get six figures at that time was a difficult task, especially since we were one of the earliest companies, and a tech company at that, to raise angel investment in Myanmar. That year, we managed to raise more than a total of US$160,000.*

That was when the business really took off. 'Starting from 5,000, 7,000, 20,000 cars a year... We were now running at 7,000 cars listed a month,' he said.

At the end of 2014, a listed Australian venture capital firm contacted CarsDB, as it was interested in expanding to emerging markets. CarsDB accepted the funding, wanting to capitalise on the global and regional advice that the venture capitalist could offer. 'We're very happy to work with them. They are helping the business to prosper as a local institution in the market,' said Wai Phyo.

Growth

While there were just three people in the team in the beginning, the team quickly expanded to include product, marketing and sales staff. However, as the listings grew to 7,000 new listings a month, CarsDB also had to scale up and build a strong service team quickly. From a team size of 10 people in 2013, the company grew to 20 people in 2014, and by 2018, it had 50 people across two offices in Yangon and Mandalay. Wai Phyo commented,

> *A lot of the work is still manual. We sometimes need to help dealers upload their car data onto the website. But this*

enables us to foster a relationship with them, by taking photos of the cars, and writing up descriptions of the car on sale, for example. Or to help them upload the perfect profile. This is how we differentiate ourselves from the competitors.

On the buyer side, many customers of CarsDB were first-time car buyers; they needed to be shown how to use the website and how to evaluate a car properly. Educating a new group of buyers about products they had never purchased before was often one of the most expensive and vexing problems marketers face. Yet, in its first year of operations, the company did not have any marketing budget to develop promotional content or attract customers.

In 2013–2014, with the expansion of the team, CarsDB could focus on building the consumer (buyer) side of the platform equation. Wai Phyo concluded,

We see more people coming to the site because their cars are selling quicker. The premium listing fee is a minimal amount compared to the margin the seller can make. Some of our dealers can make a profit of US$1,000 from each car they sell. If they sell 10 cars a month on average, US$10,000 is just pure profit.

Today, we are a fairly established brand as the number one platform for cars and car-related things, so we have 300,000 visitors every month, generating 10 million impressions for more than 10,000 cars listed for sale at any time. We're the go-to automobile buying place.

An Amazing Ride

Over time, CarsDB scaled the business by adding new services and adapting to changes based on government policies and customer needs. 'Some of our offerings are born out of demand, and some out of regulation,' added Wai Phyo. 'For example, at the end of 2013, we started partnering with insurance companies to offer car insurance because the insurance industry was liberalised. We were fortunate to be part of the journey of the insurance businesses coming into Myanmar.'

Brand New Car Segment

From late 2016 to early 2017, a more significant change in government policy took place, with a preferential shift towards smaller and safer left-hand drive vehicles instead of the previous right-hand drive ones in the market. This precipitated the opening up of a brand new car line on CarsDB, as well as facilitating buyers with bank financing to purchase these cars.

The market demand started to change towards the end of 2016. The economy was improving, and more people were buying new cars. They were also becoming familiar with used cars and the natural trajectory was that they would eventually want to buy a brand new car from the dealership or the original manufacturer. CarsDB had been supplementing its brand new car inventory since the end of 2016, and was prepared for that transition when it eventually introduced a brand new car segment on the platform. It grew out of leads for sourcing new cars that they had been receiving in the market. Wai Phyo explained,

> Myanmar is a challenging market to do business in, but the automobile sector is one of the most difficult because it involves dealing with a lot of industrial strife, manufacturing, import and export, customs, road safety and infrastructure challenges. We were fortunate to have studied different models popular in the overseas markets, so we knew what was coming and could anticipate that there would be a

demand for new cars from famous brands, for auto and liability insurance, and finance companies showing up in the market.

Service Extension — Generating and Qualifying Leads

From being the platform matching buyers and sellers, CarsDB began to provide value-added services to sellers through advertising, data analytics and sales lead qualification. The platform offered a range of services such as display advertising, and also offered cost per impression and cost per click pricing and related data to car buyers. Importantly, it also provided buyers with sales assistance — which became a part of the sales transaction. Wai Phyo said,

> *By handling inquiries and exclusions, we generate leads and link leads with car dealers, making commissions out of it. We work closely with the dealers that we partner with, allocating the leads geographically to be fair to all the dealers.*
>
> *We have a pre-sales team that will qualify leads and advise buyers about the brand model that they are looking at, and the financing options available. We explain the sales process to the customer in a very detailed manner on behalf of the dealers. Our team does all the necessary follow-ups, because in Myanmar, once you start a relationship with the service staff, customers would always want to follow up with the same person. So we handle the whole sales process.*

No matter what business model it followed, Wai Phyo believed that CarsDB was in the business of generating leads. 'We're ensuring good quality and good content at attractive, fair prices so that we can attract leads for ourselves. The same philosophy applies to anything else we do.'

New Service Lines

From 2016, CarsDB launched a succession of new service offerings in addition to the brand new car segment. For example, to facilitate lead generation, the website began to post articles, such as new product reviews before a new car was launched. 'We have a media team that covers news and articles, and reviews our upcoming or popular cars. We also cover new product launches in the market,' said Wai Phyo.

CarsDB further leveraged on technology to provide integrated solutions for the car buyer. 'For any car, since the full details of the car are on the website, we can leverage technology to automatically calculate and estimate charges for comprehensive automobile insurance. It wouldn't be possible to do this manually,' he said.

In addition, CarsDB created a membership scheme. It was a loyalty programme that gave customers preferential rates and benefits at more than 100 CarsDB after-sales service provider partners, such as auto detailing companies and service centres. 'For car sellers, we also created a three-step calculator to provide tax information such as the amount of customs duties or import taxes to pay when importing a car. We provide all the information simply and easily. Because if you look at the government websites, it's very wordy and hard to digest.'

The largest new offering, other than brand new cars on CarsDB's website, was adding e-commerce facilities for car accessories and parts, effectively incorporating a new business model. Wai Phyo commented,

We see the transition from the classified model to a more transaction-based model. That's why we are now involved

in a lot of things. Not just the cars themselves, but also in car financing and car insurance.

This is evident in CarsDB's launch of car accessories and parts, as there appears to be a ready market for it. After eight years of stocking the market with cars, there is a great need for parts, services and general maintenance. As a networked e-commerce site, companies list their products and services on the website. The margins are not so interesting for just car sales — but when you add in services and accessories, this is where the firm is growing rapidly. Having a hub where consumers, newly established garages and DIY enthusiasts come to look for products, spare parts or general information is vital in an emerging market like Myanmar, as garages and service centres have not yet been built. The new DIY owners are maintaining and servicing their vehicles and they need a trusted spot to go to for authentic and trusted materials and advice. There is a big market for parts. We are now supplying parts to 900,000 cars in the whole of Myanmar.

The Vision and the Reality

Wai Phyo was very clear about the identity that CarsDB had created over the years. 'We are the go-to place for car enthusiasts in Myanmar. Our mission is to provide one-stop information on cars and related accessories and services,' he said.

To deliver this value proposition, there were three challenges that Wai Phyo and his team faced on a daily basis. 'Number one is the people resource. Second is infrastructure, and the third is regulations.'

The greatest challenge had been finding the right talent as the company grew and scaled up its range of services. Added Wai Phyo,

The funny part is, a lot of people think it is easy to hire an accountant or a finance person. But while I know the people with the qualifications, the tough part is that they're not used to our kind of business. We have technology subscriptions, advertising and service models. We have monthly recurring revenues. They have no idea how to do revenue recognition for all that. It is stretching them and their talents. But you also need accountants to put in the controls and know what's going on in the organisation.

It is also very tough to convince people to join us. It's hard to describe CarsDB in three sentences. We are a confluence of four things: a tech-based advertising company, an online marketplace, the automobile industry and an emerging market. And you might add, an e-commerce market. So people don't understand us. In addition, a lot of people don't want to work for a small company in Myanmar. They want to go for an established traditional business. And because they can't describe CarsDB in three simple sentences, they interview, and then they don't know how to tell their friends and families what they're getting into.

Beyond that, being a tech company, we need a lot of software engineers to be able to develop our applications and website continually. We use a lot of cutting-edge technologies, and the most sophisticated tools available in the market. And that talent is not always in great supply here.

Keeping the Values that Define CarsDB

After six years in operation, Wai Phyo felt that CarsDB was still running very much like a tech startup. Reflecting on the time he had spent in the business, he commented,

It is an interesting journey to learn about an industry from scratch. Being engineers has helped my co-founders and me

to explore different fields logically, such as accounting and the sales process. The three of us have known one another for a long time. We shared a flat for seven years when we were in Singapore, and we are still good friends now.

We would always want to keep the core culture of being a tech startup. From day one, we've made decisions really fast, because we believe that this is better than making slow ones. Even though we are now a team of 50 people, we keep all the communication channels very open and transparent, and ultimately we try to leverage technology tools to facilitate our day-to-day operations.

Also, we are focused around integrity and ethics... When you sell advertising to a company, and they give me US$5,000, how would they know what they have bought? By getting a report to show where we have displayed US$5,000 worth of advertising on our wall or in terms of impressions. So, we regard high ethics and high integrity as a top priority. Even though it's a non-tangible, technology solution that we're selling, we want to ensure that everything we're doing is correct and proper.

2017 and Beyond

Starting from scratch, CarsDB had managed to grow to become the biggest online car platform in Myanmar in less than five years. Their innovative business model, coupled with their quick response to regulatory changes, had helped disrupt the traditional sales method, augment the consumer experience and shape the buying process for an entire industry.

In 2017, CarsDB held the largest auto show in Myanmar, inviting all of their corporate clients to attend. Before that, they had hosted close to 15 small-scale local industry events, to foster closeness in the community. The auto show, with both new and used cars on display, brought together members from OEMs, brands, new and used car dealers, and parts and service suppliers. Wai Phyo recalled,

> *We had about 20,000 people that came to the first event in Yangon over two days. They bought over 300 cars in just two days. The second event we did in Mandalay was over three days. We sold about 500 cars, and had about 13,000 people coming across. It was the largest and most challenging event that we have ever done.*

This highly visible and publicised event was the last piece of the puzzle for Wai Phyo in becoming the official body that united the automobile community in Myanmar. To jumpstart an industry, it often takes a spark. CarsDB appears to be the flame that has ignited the growth in the automobile business in Myanmar. It has helped create a platform that connects buyers and sellers of cars, insurance, parts, accessories and servicing, while providing readily accessible information on financing, taxes and other inquiries.

A competitive advantage is developed by these activities that a firm performs, which provides it with a relative strength when compared to its competitors. These advantages are often the result of not one activity, a silver bullet if you will — the most unassailable competitive positions are the result of a series of steps that have been executed in totality and are thus very difficult to copy or replicate. The path undertaken and executed by the founders and management of CarsDB have put them at the forefront of a rapidly developing industry with a very bright future.

Chapter 9

NEXLABS: PIVOTING TO HELP CUSTOMERS CREATE AND CAPTURE VALUE

Our DNA is about looking for opportunities to automate operations or develop elegant solutions that help our customers create and capture value.

— Ye Myat Min, CEO & Founder, Nexlabs

Nexlabs was one of the leading tech companies in Myanmar with about 90 employees as of 2018. It offered value-creating solutions for clients looking to solve their supply chain and e-commerce issues with technology. Nexlabs was headed by Ye Myat Min, recognised as one of Forbes Asia's '30 Under 30' in 2016.

It was not a straightforward journey for Nexlabs to get where it was, and Ye Myat had to pivot the company's original business proposition several times in order to survive in the still small but rapidly evolving tech market that characterised Myanmar.

Background

Ye Myat was born to be a software engineer. He shared,

I've been a software engineer my entire life. I started programming at the age of 12 in Myanmar, so that's pretty much the only thing I know how to do. I didn't have much of a high school life. I was happily playing computer games and trying to write programmes for games, etc.

Growing up in Myanmar, educational options were limited. Ye Myat recalled,

When I turned 16, I had a choice to go to Singapore for further studies, or join the medical school here. Because the education system in Myanmar was not that fantastic back in the day, the only choice you really had was medical school.

While many of his friends went on to become doctors, Ye Myat followed his passion for software engineering, which brought him to Singapore. There he enrolled in Republic Polytechnic (RP), which had a teaching style that suited his personality. He elaborated,

I joined RP because of its different teaching methodology. It is a programme-based approach. And for someone who loved self-studying like I did, that was the perfect methodology. I don't like just learning from the blackboard; I had had enough of that in Myanmar.

Republic Polytechnic

Ye Myat balanced work and fun during his time at Republic Polytechnic — he used to hang out at the nearby arcade playing games with his schoolmates. Importantly, it also gave him the opportunity to work on a few freelance projects where he could collaborate with others, which is how he started his career in software engineering early, at age 17.

Ye Myat took on projects for several restaurants and small enterprises, building their websites and apps. While these jobs helped to pay for his school fees and living expenses in Singapore, it also exposed him to some of the challenges businesses faced. He recalled,

> *When I got into the advertising industry, we were still using Friendster and Myspace and a lot of other names that aren't around any more. But the opportunity was really around digital, new media. Facebook was on the horizon. Instagram was just starting up. And Apple had announced the App Store. Initially when Apple launched the iPhone, there was no App Store, but when it announced the development of the platform, I got into that and started building apps for people.*

With the advertising industry at the forefront of technology, brands were finding different avenues of marketing to consumers. Ye Myat observed,

> *Luckily for me I had all the technical skills that I had picked up along the way, so I went in that direction during school. And the rest is basically history.*

Going to University

After graduating from Republic Polytechnic, Ye Myat planned to work for an advertising agency as a full-time employee, but his parents would not hear of it. He explained,

> *They told me, 'We've spent so much money getting you into Singapore and getting you an education, now just go attend a university.' Because that's what you did. All my cousins had a degree. It was mandatory. At the time, I thought I've done technology for my whole life and I want to pick up*

something that I haven't done before, which is business. Also, I was reading TechCrunch and all these technology blogs where you see kids from say Silicon Valley, California, picking up venture capital funding when they were only 19 or 20. I was quite inspired by that and thought that I should pick up some business skills.

Ye Myat initially applied to the School of Business at Singapore Management University (SMU), but he did not get in. So he joined SMU's School of Information Systems to study Information System Management, hoping to do a minor in business.

The first two semesters in SMU were horrible because I was working. Frankly, I just didn't have time for school. But without the work, I wouldn't be able to pay tuition fees for SMU in any case. It was a balancing act and unfortunately, since I never really wanted to go to university, I chose work. My grades were horrendous and I got two warning letters in the first semester.

Video Streaming

In 2012, during his second year at university, Ye Myat co-founded a video streaming startup in Singapore. 'That was way before anyone was doing video streaming,' he said. However, the startup didn't do very well. Ye Myat reflected on the key takeaways,

We got involved with the wrong type of investors. It was stressful, but it also taught me a lot. Investment is not always good. You need to be very careful about who you take money from. Sometimes there are unreasonable expectations as to when the payouts are going to come and how much risk they're actually assuming. Especially in technology, the pay-off is a long-term game. It's never going to be in a year or two years, rather it's going to be more like, five to 10 years.

[In watching management] I learned a little bit more about leadership and how transparency is really the key. You can't misrepresent certain information to your colleagues and your employees and, in a way, deceive them. They will find out. It was one of the early lessons on what we should not be doing when running a company.

The other lesson that I learned was around product market fit. You could be doing all this fancy stuff but will not succeed if the market isn't ready for it. We were doing video streaming in Singapore at a time when people wouldn't necessarily want to stream video because data was expensive, so we never got traction. And we spent so much time — actually, we spent six months in R&D — trying to make it perfect. Although design-wise and technically it was perfect, from the consumer point of view, it was never perfect. There wasn't any use case around it.

As the founding team, we were working under no or minimal salary terms. Later, we found out that there was an intern who was paid a salary above the market rate. Was there something fishy going on? When you find out things like this, it just irks you and demotivates you. There is strength in common sacrifice for the greater good, but finding out that the sacrifice was not common or equal was demoralising for the team.

Nexlabs

Having gained experience from his failed venture, Ye Myat began to conceive the idea for what would eventually become Nexlabs. He went on leave of absence from the university, and eventually did not graduate, using the time to focus on developing the business that was officially incorporated in 2013.

Mobile App Builder

Ye Myat recognised that apps, especially smartphone apps, were taking over the world.

> *I knew that was going to come and someday it was going to come into Myanmar. I just didn't know that it would happen so quickly, because Myanmar was then still a very closed country — SIM cards cost $2,000 at that time. Then 4G came along and the price of SIM cards dropped a lot. These are the kinds of things that enable a market. It's transformative in a lot of ways.*

Ye Myat started Nexlabs in April 2013 as a product studio.

> *We were trying to build an e-commerce platform, very similar to what Shopify at the time was doing. They were building ready-made e-commerce websites for anyone who wanted to sell stuff online. We were doing the same thing, but for apps. We constructed a mobile app builder, so once you uploaded your products onto a platform, you got a mobile app with your brand name on top of it.*

It seemed like a good idea at the time, because people in Myanmar had started using smartphones, which were becoming increasingly cheaper. The number of Internet users was also increasing. Facebook was very popular among users and there was a rising number of online shops on the platform, which were, however, doing everything manually. Ye Myat thought that his platform would be a good way to automate a lot of things.

> *The product was good. But I made the same mistake again — we made the product too perfect. We spent about*

eight to 10 months trying to figure out the right product and the technical aspects of it, but we didn't test pricing.

We were all a bunch of engineers. I consider myself to be a pure software engineer. I failed accounting. I didn't like economics. I didn't like statistics. So we were just kicking around in a small shared office. And when we finally launched it into the world, nobody bought it. As a result, we never really shipped it out of the door to customers.

Software Subscription

At the same time, Nexlabs was testing out a software as a subscription (SaaS) business model, charging US$17 a month to each merchant for access to the product studio. 'In our minds, we were thinking, 'this is so cheap considering the benefits it provides — why wouldn't you buy it?' But the merchants were unwilling to pay for the software, even though they were willing to use it if it were given for free,' he said.

The product launch, though a failure, gave Ye Myat valuable insights into the market. Although e-commerce was growing, online payments were tricky as Myanmar was still very much a cash-on-delivery economy. Less than one percent of the population used credit cards at the time, not to mention how difficult it was to obtain a credit card in the first place. Debit cards were used by less than five percent of the population. It would be hard to implement any e-commerce model without a way to take payment.

Secondly, the country lacked adequate infrastructure for logistics and transportation. Automation was not the pain point for merchants; their actual pain points were in getting the product delivered to the customer and in the event of a cash-on-delivery transaction, collecting payment. These were enormous challenges.

Much like his past experience in the streaming market, Nexlabs' technology was good, but the market fit was poor. Limited financial inclusion and a gap in logistical infrastructure again led to a product ahead of its market.

International Funding

A big part of the success of companies like Lazada, an e-commerce platform, was that they were able to follow a cash-on-delivery model. But this model was very capital-intensive — such funding for startups, say to the tune of US$40 or US$50 million, would be impossible to raise in emerging markets such as Myanmar. Between the current scale and the investment laws, a large-scale capital-intensive business model was very tough to initiate and execute. Ye Myat elaborated,

> If you are operating out of Myanmar, and you don't have any track record or any ecosystem around you, it's impossible to get a sizeable amount of funding. International investors are thinking about their confidence in the market and also about getting their money into and out of the country. This is why so many other companies are incorporated in Singapore. We did the same.

Anonymous Social Networks

The lack of market readiness and funding for the product studio made it imperative for the business and the accompanying business model to change. Nexlab's first pivot from the existing business came in the form of a social media network. Around 2015, anonymous social networks such as Whisper and Secret were gaining popularity in the United States. Ye Myat and his team tested the model in Myanmar, and within two weeks, they had more than 10,000 users. It was a tremendous success and the future looked bright.

But two weeks later, the government questioned Nexlabs about the appearance of hate speech and pornography on the platform. While the social network was growing, Nexlabs' content moderation team could not handle the high volume. Ye Myat said, 'They called and asked me politely to turn off the service. That was a depressing time when we had to shut down the servers.' Worse still, many core team members then left Nexlabs because they felt the company was drifting toward a different direction from when it was founded, and they didn't agree with that.

> *One of the key lessons at that point was that the founders should communicate every problem that they are facing, because if you don't, the team will not understand. I think what I did wrong was to try to shield everything bad and only communicate the good stuff to the team because I wanted to motivate them. Bad news is a heavy weight on their shoulders, but on the flip side, if you don't communicate the bad stuff, nobody will know that there are imperatives.*
>
> *We lost pretty much half of the 16 people in our team. That's when we went back to the drawing board and started figuring out how to stay in this game for the longer term. Because if there's no capital, if there's no cash flow, then your ideas are worth nothing. You need to stay in business long enough to get things to reach fruition.*

Given the major setback that Ye Myat experienced in the business, there was a need to step back and reassess where the business was heading and how to build it yet again.

Back to the Drawing Board

2016 was a year of self-discovery and rediscovery for the firm. Nexlabs began to look inwards at its strengths and weaknesses, and out to the market to see where the opportunities were.

> *We went back to what we knew. We started to recognise that because of our past experience, we now have a skill. And the skill is to understand the commercial process between production and consumption. We had gleaned valuable insights and learnings from developing products for business-to-business and business-to-consumer models. The consumer research we had done and our insight into the user experience, design- and customer-led approaches were quite valuable and became the core of our business.*
>
> *We used all these insights to start helping other people build products and avoid some of the traps that we had fallen into. This is where we started to gain traction — helping people to get from here to there. We were able to offer assistance to people who were looking to start their businesses, get their businesses off the ground and grow the business.*

The Evolution of Nexlabs

As Nexlabs evolved, it slowly crystallised its identity. It took about a year for it to solidify its position as an e-commerce platform. However, in its DNA, Nexlabs was a firm that took a consultative approach to assisting managers in understanding and constructing the core processes of their businesses through better data insights. Their platforms enabled a learning and evolving firm to shine.

A bulk of Nexlabs's business involved looking into the clients' business processes to see how it could be automated. The company also analysed its clients' value chains to reveal pain points and customise solutions. It did so by figuring out the data points the company needed to capture, how to extract the data, and how to use this data to help clients make better decisions. The platform was customised for each company and gave them visibility into their business activities, enabling them to make corrections and modifications, and use it to manage their organisation. Ye Myat confessed,

> *I love helping entrepreneurs and family businesses transition to online businesses. We helped a brick-and-mortar retail chain open an e-commerce store. We're actually working with City Mart (a local supermarket chain) at the moment on two projects — customer loyalty and online commerce. It has a more consumer-facing aspect; understanding the user experience and what consumers need, and conducting consumer research. We've got a mix of backend, internal-facing and external-facing projects that we handle.*

Building Nexlabs

Having reoriented the company's mission in 2016, Ye Myat concentrated on fundraising, ensuring that there was cash in the bank, rebuilding a project pipeline and rebuilding his team.

It was during that round of fundraising that Ye Myat learnt an important lesson about fundraising.

> *A major mistake — and I will never do this again — was that we did a handshake deal. It was very hard to get foreign investment here and we did not want to set up a Singapore company. So all of the funds were transferred into my*

personal account in Myanmar. All was fine until we found an institutional investor later on and this came up during their due diligence process. That cost us a lot of money to solve, paying out to lawyers, etc. That was a lesson; we'll never do that again.

Nexlabs raised close to a million dollars by 2018 from local investors as well as institutional investors from Singapore (including a Myanmar tech fund based in Singapore). Ye Myat said,

Fundraising is never easy, but it is fun. I like fundraising because it kind of makes you think hard about the future. You have got to sell the vision and you need to figure out what the vision is. I joke about this with my guys. My usage of computers has changed. The first three years in the company I was building and designing the product. The last two years I've just been on Excel. I get a little bit of guilty pleasure here and there trying to code some stuff, but they don't like me coding stuff. I'm spending time on Excel and PowerPoint.

Hiring the Right People

As the business got on the right trajectory in late 2016, Ye Myat spent a lot of time straightening out his team. He did not make wise choices initially, admitting, 'We made a couple of wrong hires at times, so we wasted time without focusing on the business.'

Much of the company's business was on a project-by-project basis. As such, Nexlabs faced the age-old problem of consulting companies, one of having the right number of people for projects on hand. 'It's easy to get into those spontaneous decisions where you need people to close the deal, so you hire people. But then when the project ends, what do you do with those people?'

In early 2016, being stretched between having to hire, run operations and find commercial deals, Ye Myat finally hired a person who would run the commercial side of the business, to meet the company's increasing demand for technology. 'I started handing everything over to him in terms of commercial activities. That was a key moment in our history when we prepared to scale up. Then the business started growing,' he said.

Growth was also about market timing. Before 2016, few customers were interested in leveraging technology to improve their business, instead choosing to spend their dollars in gaining advertising reach for their products. But by late 2016, companies in Myanmar gradually became more receptive to integrating technology into their businesses. That was when Nexlabs really started growing from its team of 25–30 people.

2017 became Nexlabs's best year ever — revenues grew 300% from the previous year. That year, the team too grew to about 80 people. Key milestones achieved during this time included building the right team and implementing a middle management structure. Ye Myat explained,

> Up until late 2016, we had a structure in which everybody reported to me. With a team of 50, 60 or 80 people, I just couldn't do it any more. One of our investors [Magnus Bocker, former head of the Singapore Stock Exchange] suggested a 30-90-300 structure, where at 30 people, we would create a new management layer; at 90 people another layer; and at 300, we would have multiple layers, and so on as we scaled.

Ye Myat spent most of his time in 2017 on HR-related issues, most importantly hiring the right people for technical and managerial positions. He managed to hire some expatriates who had worked with Internet tech companies such as Amazon and Rocket Internet into key positions at Nexlabs. The management team was empowered to make its own decisions, subverting the owner-led approach that was predominant in Myanmar where it was typically the founder/owner who called all the shots.

A bigger challenge was the supply of talent in Myanmar. Having virtually no private enterprise a decade earlier, finding the right people was incredibly hard. He explained,

> *You just don't have a cadre of people who have an understanding of what a manager does. And the other thing that was really hard for us was finding technical people. So we had to find both managers and engineers. We were interviewing a person a day and just kept on interviewing.*
>
> *One key lesson that we've reflected on in 2018 is that we hired too quickly. It's always easy to hire, but it's always very hard to fire. Also in a country like Myanmar, employees are actually really protected. You can't do immediate dismissals or downsizing, it is a cumbersome process.*

Ye Myat recognised that Nexlabs was basically a consultancy business with a linear business model, which, although profitable, would not experience exponential growth like other product tech companies. That is, as the number of jobs grew, the number of new employees needed to execute those projects tracked that growth.

> *We realised that there's always going to be a correlation between the number of people we have and the amount of business opportunities and projects out there. Expenses in Myanmar grow very quickly, especially human capital costs. It's still our number one cost because of the limited talent pool available here. The price of that talent increases every*

year. They go from job to job if they are talented. They can
double their salary in a year, just like that.

Tweaking Strategy and Forging Partnerships

Going forward, Ye Myat felt that Nexlabs did not need to pivot its business model but, rather, tweak its current business strategy to maintain a steady cash flow with an eye to capturing more of the value it created.

> *We're going in the direction of capitalising on our assets, our human assets, and creating more value out of them — not just by taking in more work, but figuring out how to capture the upside of the products that we build for our clients.*

More directly, Nexlabs was looking at drawing up new contract terms with a number of clients to share the intellectual property on a results basis, rather than fee for service. That is, they sought to sell the product to companies that required such a solution, and being compensated on the impact rather than a mark-up on time and materials.

Working with retailers also allowed Nexlabs to look into providing data analytics and consumer insights to retailers, retail channels and manufacturers. These solutions would help businesses figure out what they could do to increase sales transactions, with Nexlabs possibly getting a share of that revenue. 'It's a little more exciting than what we have been doing because it's a mix of commercial terms and understanding of the product and the market. It takes a combination of all three to figure out where we can capture the best value.'

The challenge for Nexlabs was to persuade customers, who may be conservative in their approach, to new ways of doing business and to partake in these new business models. However, there could be countless partnership opportunities in areas such as enabling money transfer between banks and online payments for utility bills.

> *We know that in Myanmar we can't do this alone, because we don't have unlimited capital like that in Silicon Valley. We have to find the capital. In choosing these new opportunities, I'm looking out for people who share the same passion and the same values about collaboration and co-creation. That's really the basis of my hypothesis. And through working with some of these institutions such as City Mart, we know it is going to be very insightful because we're not retail guys. We're just a bunch of geeks, but we know about data and how important it is. If we meshed these values together, I think that's really where the new exciting opportunities are... I think that's really where the future is, especially around co-creation, because right now there is very little technology being used in the market. Everywhere you look, there is so much opportunity to start using technology and increase efficiency.*

Ye Myat reflected on the path travelled so far with a mixture of marvel and clarity,

> *This idea of what we do now started a year and a half ago, in the beginning of 2017. But it could not have been achieved had we not gone through the journey. We have pivoted multiple times in the past to reach where we are today.*
>
> *Today, we help medium-sized and large enterprises solve their business challenges by using technology. The problem can be from virtually any domain. If you have issues around payroll and HR management or inventory*

management, we try to come up with creative technological solutions to solve these problems. And we also build consumer-facing products. For example, we're helping one of the large retail chains in Myanmar to establish their e-commerce channels. In summary, we help our clients use technology for three main things: to grow their revenue, to increase their efficiency and to operate better.

However, the next stage is always just ahead on the horizon.

To me, it's not a business if you're not progressing. My pivots have been a way of progression, so I think there will definitely be pivots in the future. The challenge really is how you pivot 90 people. One of the things about Myanmar is there are so many attractive opportunities, that as an entrepreneur, you tend to want to go after all of them, but focus is going to be the key.

The future for Nexlabs looks bright as each pivot has led to enhanced understandings and insights into the challenges managers encounter and the commonality of the hurdles faced. As Myanmar continues to grow, formalise and move toward international standards, there is still a need for professional management to be equipped with the tools that enable them to perform at their best. The intersection among resources, opportunities, skills and the tools that enable efficient and effective execution never seems to go out of style.

Chapter 10

FLYMYA — DOING GOOD FOR THE COUNTRY WHILE FLYING HIGH

I want to change the country and make an impact.

— Mike Than Tun Win, Flymya's CEO and founder

Mike's success working in a non-tech-related business had encouraged and propelled him to want to take part in the liberalisation of Myanmar's industries and the tech opportunities that came with it.

Flymya started as an online travel portal selling flight and bus tickets, but quickly expanded to include ticketing for events and attractions as well as business-to-business (B2B) services. As an Internet-based business, it delivered the online platform as well as the hardware that connected sellers and buyers, providing a means for payment in a market that was predominantly cash-based.

By early 2019, the company had grown to about 160 people, after a whirlwind two and a half years of operations. It had also diversified into a plethora of services that stayed true to Mike's mission of improving financial inclusivity in Myanmar and facilitating the country's economic growth. However, the pieces of the puzzle were just coming together to form a much bigger picture.

Early Days

Mike did not set out to be a tech entrepreneur, and in fact he took a roundabout route getting there. Graduating from Nanyang Technological University in Singapore with a degree in business in 2008, he met a director of an oil company, who told him about a booming opportunity in Vietnam. Mike added,

> *I was just a crazy young kid. I got to know this regional director in the oil industry, who said, 'Vietnam is opening up, and there is a big motorcycle boom. I've already tried to trade some products there; you can supply me with some products.' So, I went in because I had just graduated. And why not? I just wanted to put myself into a very new environment.*

Mike ended up spending 18 months in Vietnam, which allowed him to understand the automotive and lubricants market well. The venture was not financially successful, but he learnt some hard lessons during that period, unfortunately losing a lot of money in the process.

Looking back, Mike reflected, 'Probably if I had not started to do business in Vietnam, I wouldn't have had the later success in Myanmar. So I might have been paying for that lesson in Myanmar instead of in Vietnam. It's just a matter of where and when.'

During his time in Vietnam, Mike also invested US$100,000 into a lubricant company in Bangkok, Thailand. The company is still operating today. 'We have good partners in Bangkok, the company is quite successful today.'

His experience in lubricants enabled him to apply his knowledge back home in Myanmar and capitalise on the opportunity that presented itself. He said,

In 2011, we had about 200,000 cars in a nation of 55 million people. So, I thought that the new government would definitely open up the automotive sector. But being an automobile importer involves high capital. So again, I thought, why don't we trade in automotive products like lubricants, filters and aftermarket services? And I started a small company of about 30 people to do that.

The company, which Mike owned with his cousins, earned about US$1 million in revenue in its first year, which was considered a significant achievement for a small enterprise in Myanmar.

In 2012, the automotive industry in Myanmar started to open up, and in 2013, sanctions were officially lifted. Car prices dropped dramatically in the space of a year, because there were no more quotas placed on car imports. A car that used to cost US$300,000 could suddenly cost as little as US$30,000. What was formerly a luxury good was now affordable and a demand boom was set off. 'The number of automobiles grew almost threefold in the next three years. Because of the boom, every kind of car-related consumption increased. Lubricants, batteries, tyres, you name it,' said Mike.

In January 2016, the company was sold to a listed company in Singapore. Mike remained semi-involved in the business. 'By then we already had a 20% market share for lubricant products in Myanmar. We supplied to almost every power station, and exclusively supplied to some luxury car brands,' he said.

With a measure of success under his belt by the time he was 30, what made Mike decide to, figuratively, 'climb another mountain' and found a new business? He recalled,

I think it's a personal choice. I want to change the country. I want to really make an impact. Lots of industries are going

to evolve rapidly in this country and I want to help make it happen. For instance, we had a huge telco boom in less than two years because the government fully privatised it. So as I see the world evolving, I thought I should be part of it; I am a part of it. I wanted to find a market niche that can help bring things to the people of Myanmar.

Founding Flymya

In 2015, Mike decided to open a technology startup with a friend. He registered the travel portal Flymya, and the company went live in January 2016.

Flymya started out with the aim of becoming a full service travel website and aggregator, offering flights and bus tickets for sale from different merchants. Mike elaborated,

> *Something like a travel portal is quite uncommon in Southeast Asia as online travel agencies in other countries are usually more sector-focused — flights or hotels only, tours only or car rental. We decided to offer all of these right from the beginning. Of course, this approach also made us much more capital-intensive regarding the R&D, IT development and investments required.*

The profits from the trading business were what enabled Mike to fund Flymya initially.

> *I had 35% ownership, with the remaining 65% owned by my cousins. With this type of funding structure, I ran Flymya almost like a traditional startup with equity funding.*
> *I had started Flymya with one of my friends from Singapore in 2015, but unfortunately, he burned out after about a year. Things were not going right that first year, and my friend couldn't take it in Myanmar any more — the*

developers were leaving, turnover was high, he faced language barriers; he was just not comfortable here. So, he quit. That is why I came in to manage the business. Initially, he held a 40 percent founder's equity, and with our cash funding, my cousins and I got the other 60 percent. After he left, we bought over his initial investment and compensated him for his time. Then we owned the business 100 percent, and in 2016 I really had to roll up my sleeves and look at the business. I truly became an entrepreneur.

The year 2015 was spent getting the house in order; hiring people, getting licenses and working with partners. In an entrepreneurial journey, you could say, this was a time when the rubber was about to meet the road. When the Flymya website officially went live in January 2016, the company's focus was only on attracting usage from foreigners wanting to visit Myanmar. Mike explained,

We were handling about US$1.5 million worth of tickets in sales once our website went live, and we earned about US$120,000 revenue in the first month. We only had about 15 people back then. As a small team we were encouraged. We realised that there existed a pain point in foreign travel, else it would not have been possible to bring in that much revenue so quickly. But by the end of 2016, we also came to realise that we could not just count on foreigners; the revenue was too low. So, in 2017, we turned our attention to the local Burmese market. That was when we had a huge breakthrough in terms of revenue, market share and the concept of what our business was.

The strategy to pivot towards local consumers worked, and in 2017, Flymya experienced a more than threefold jump in revenue. 'This year [2018] we should be definitely making more than seven-digit US dollars in revenue monthly, which is about 8 percent of the total market share for domestic flight tickets,' he said.

By 2018, Mike spent 80–85 percent of his time running his tech businesses.

Leveraging the Flymya Platform to Extend B2B Reach and Services

Mike said,

> Along the way, we're putting things together, we're working with our retailers. We start to see these enablers coming together; things like telco prices coming down, and the ability to have electronic wallets and stuff. And then we start to think, let's pivot. We're not going to be just a travel portal. We're going to move beyond that... into omnichannel.

The Flymya website gradually started to have comprehensive offerings for travel packages, free and easy travel, as well as non-travel ticketing. For each type of ticketing, Flymya worked differently with its partners to ensure that its tech platform catered to the partners' needs.

Tour Packages

Mike recollected,

> What we did first was launch something like an eBay for the tour. If you look at other Online-Tour-Agencies (OTAs), they have maybe 100 packages in their catalogue. We have more than 1,000 packages.

Flymya created accounts for more than 200 travel agents, enabling them to list their own packages and offer their content online through the Flymya platform. This applied to both inbound (day tours), and outbound (for example, a trip to Japan) travel to and from Myanmar, respectively. 'We opened up the platform, and every travel agent went online to list. We charge about 3% commission for each sale, but we supplied the eyeballs,' he said.

Through this partnership method with OTAs, Flymya also helped launch numerous FIT (Free Independent Traveller or Free Independent Tourist) tours, which constituted selling flights and hotel packages to travellers who preferred to travel free and easy.

Mike added, 'The FIT is pretty successful for us. It's cheaper to buy a package from us [compared to buying the hotel and flights separately on your own].'

Subagents

Flymya also innovated with its platform to offer a B2B system to empower the small travel agent to access the global marketplace for hotels and flights. Previously, small travel agents would go to global travel websites such as Booking.com to purchase a hotel stay, and charge a mark-up from there that they would pass on to their customer. It was an inefficient and costly process. The travel agents would also have to place deposits with these providers directly. Mike said,

> *The idea was that Flymya would connect directly to the hotel global distribution system. We would then link up these small travel agents, who could sell any of these hotels on their own. We'd charge them a base price of 3 percent of gross price. Then anything that the travel agent charged above that would be their own margin. By us handling the global distribution system, we were able to reduce the headroom for local agents as platforms would charge 15 percent gross price on a hotel. On the other side, for*

> *supplying a booking, we are generally getting about 12–15%*
> *of gross price.*

The travel agents effectively became subagents on the Flymya portal. Through the Flymya B2B dashboard, they would be able to issue bus and flight tickets and car rental vouchers. They would keep a deposit only with Flymya, which could be topped up on a regular basis. The dashboard would enable them to keep track of their real-time balances with Flymya. 'Now every travel agent here can easily sell hotel stays in Singapore to their walk-in customers,' said Mike.

Ticketing Travel to Ticketing Lifestyles

With all these linkages being built up with service providers, Flymya began to branch out into being a platform offering tickets for local and international attractions and events, such as zoo or concert tickets. In 2017, Flymya successfully "powered" about 100,000 event tickets through its event-ticketing app for events companies. Mike recalled,

> *In most countries with event ticketing websites, they have*
> *an old legacy system with point of sales (POS) ticket printing*
> *systems. We went fully online into the cloud. Everything is*
> *run through an app that can generate quick response or QR*
> *codes for e-tickets. Every event organiser gets a dashboard*
> *to manage the event tickets. Event organisers would use our*
> *app to scan and verify the e-ticket for entry. They did not*
> *have to invest in heavy machines any more.*
>
> *As an OTA, rightly, we shouldn't be doing event ticketing.*
> *We've become more of a lifestyle service because people*
> *come to us for solutions. They say, 'We have a party, could*
> *you help sell tickets for us?' Then we look at it and say, 'The*

ticket is hard to deliver because it's not digital. So why don't we digitalise it for you?'

It hasn't been easy as we are forced to think about things very differently in this market, given the lack of digital literacy, banking services or entrenched consumer behaviour. So, we have to be creative. And step-by-step, we realised that we are doing things pretty differently from other OTAs because we have to morph into this market. Our solution has to fit the context of the market, or more directly, the state of its development.

Accessing the Unbanked

While Mike grew his business, he kept foremost in his mind a social mission to help in the country's economic development. It was also the root of a lot of innovation that Flymya undertook in response to the market environment. Mike said,

In Myanmar, things are very different. Most countries have telcos and financial instruments, such as banking and credit cards, which develop in parallel. In this country, we have very weak GDP and financial inclusion. We cannot repeat the success of Silicon Valley, or even China, in the same way. The bankable population is less than 30%.

We have 35 million telco subscriptions, but the number of active SIMs is closer to 55 million because some people use two SIMs. But in comparison, the country has only about 200,000 credit cards issued. If we depended purely on online payments and traditional fulfilment like cash on delivery, we would limit our growth a lot. As we started to court the Burmese consumer in 2017, we realised within the first six to eight months that payment was a big problem for the Burmese. We talked to the banks about their plans to roll out more financially inclusive services, and I thought, if I wait for them, I'll probably be dead. So I decided to bypass the need for a bank account and digitalise all our assets.

The Omnichannel POS Terminal

Mike added,

We've successfully digitalised bus and flight tickets, and tours from fragmented vendors, and connected them through database management onto our portal. We have become a single source for all of these services. The result of this process is that we have created what we call the 'omnichannel' terminal.

If you asked me in 2016, I wouldn't have thought of that. If you asked us in 2017, just last year, maybe in January, I wouldn't have thought of that. I was just busy trying to approach the Burmese market. But we started to realise the payment pain point, and we needed to solve it. Who knows, maybe in one years' time there might be new pain points that we will need to solve.

After taking the effort to connect the disparate vendors onto the Flymya platform, Mike set out to empower small mom-and-pop shops by providing them with terminals to sell these tickets. The terminals, to be linked to Flymya's travel portal, had been tested in the market for two months.

From a single terminal, looking like a typical credit card swipe machine, mom-and-pop shops would be able to search for, sell, as well as print, flight tickets, bus tickets and mobile telephone top-ups. Customers could fill in their personal information on the terminal's screen to purchase tickets, which they would then pay for in cash.

The mom-and-pop stores would earn a 5 percent commission for every ticket that they sold. For the merchants, Flymya would share half the commission with them for each sale. More empowering however, the mom-and-pop shop that was located in the neighbourhood could now offer these new services for sale and provide the local convenience for neighbourhood customers who were often unbanked. This could produce a platform for virtually endless aisles. The possibilities were limitless.

To operate the terminal system, retailers had to first top-up a virtual account with Flymya to an amount of at least US$300. To make up for the USD/MMK exchange rate differences, Flymya granted the retailer a five percent discount off the ticket price when it was deducted from the retailer's wallet. For example, if the customer paid the retailer MMK 5,000 for a ticket, the Flymya system would automatically deduct MMK 4,750 from the retailer's virtual wallet. The retailer, then had MKK 250 net margin in hand.

The terminal also served as a POS device that was connected to all the banks, where the virtual wallet sat on the Flymya bank dashboard. 'The retailers do not have to sign on to multiple gateways any more. They don't have to go through the hassle of opening bank accounts and having individual POS machines to collect MPU [Myanmar Payment Union], Visa and mobile payments. It's all credited to their virtual wallet,' said Mike.

Consumers were now able to transact with retailers on a cash basis, doing away with a need for a bank account or credit card to buy tickets online. There would also be no need to travel further than the local mom-and-pop store to make the purchase. Telcos, bus companies, airlines etc., were also happy with the concept because they had greatly expanded their distribution by more than 60,000 retail points across Myanmar. Mike said,

So this approach is pretty unique to Myanmar because, in some countries, nobody pays in cash any more. Everybody goes directly to the respective merchant's website and pays with their credit card. But people don't trust that so much here, and it's also not readily available.

The idea that every mom-and-pop shop can sell a bus ticket or a hotel stay and get a five percent commission makes them immediately a multi-product retailer. This is part of the digital revolution. Most digital revolutions tend to want to keep them (small local retailers) out, but they have become a part of it.

The sign-up rate with retailers is about 50 percent. The app was built by us, while the terminal is manufactured in China. We are thinking of maybe licensing it or exporting it as a software solution one day.

In 2018, Flymya was developing a POS 'lite' version that would be purely mobile app-based, for retailers to sell smaller ticket items such as bus tickets and utility bills, requiring a retailer wallet with a lower top-up fee of US$100. This was expected to help the rural penetration rates where incomes are much lower, and banking penetration is almost non-existent.

About Adoption

Mike understood that the adoption of his solution was strongly grounded in the local culture and consumer behaviour. He said,

In Myanmar, no matter how deep we are in digital penetration, we need to give consumers some time to adopt new products. And being an Asian country, it's always easier through word of mouth in your social circle. So long as we have a mom-and-pop shop covering 10 streets, consumers don't mind listening to a new idea. If you've seen this person in your neighbourhood for the last 10 years and he says, 'Hey, I got a new thing. Would you like to try it? Why not buy a ticket from me?' You might just try it once.

Mike paused to reflect,

Many distribution channels don't look at the social trust issue, and digital products always have trust issues surrounding them. Especially in developing countries. You are flooded with a lot of information and social media — how do you make a wise decision? How do you trust it? And you can't touch it, right? People are still tactile at the end of the day.

Social Good

Mike commented, 'I see small tech startups and young people struggling. I always think — why not allocate some budget to these companies?' In 2016, Flymya started investing in other companies through a venture capital company they formed called BODTech. BODTech aimed to fund the digital revolution in Myanmar by investing in Internet companies with potential.

Investments were given to the founders of different companies with few strings attached. Mike said,

A few of the startups that we have invested in are pretty strong. We took 50 percent equity in Yangon Door2Door, a tiny food delivery company back in 2016. Today, it is Myanmar's number one online food ordering and delivery service, with more than 90 percent of the industry market share, hosting menus from a wide range of Yangon's most popular restaurants. The interesting thing about Myanmar is that most franchise chains here do not do deliveries on their own any more. In most countries, the fast food chains do their own fulfilments, but here they work exclusively with Yangon Door2Door.

In February 2018, another BODTech investment, Spree.com.mm, became the first e-commerce business to launch a microfinance plus e-commerce package for consumers. Consumers would be able to buy products online and apply for a loan at the cheapest interest rate in the country. 'Consumers would buy online, apply for the loan online and receive the product at home. And they would fill out a loan paper, print it and send it in,' said Mike.

The Cost of Doing Business

The increasing variety of Flymya's business services had also meant that in just over 10 years, the company had grown from just eight people to over 160. This was quite an expansion for a digitally based firm that specialised in making transactions seamless and easy.

'Nowadays, people know us more as a tech company than a travel one. Of course, travel is still our biggest portfolio,' said Mike.

He observed that the relatively lower cost of doing business in Myanmar was one critical factor that had made such growth possible.

You can test a concept or even make a mistake without it being fatal. The advantage here is that the Myanmar marketplace requires a much lower level of capital expenditure. If you start a business in Singapore, and you don't get things right in the first year, you've got to shut the shop immediately. But here we have more room for trial and error. Nobody is the smartest guy on the block. Nobody will get things right on the first day. You might be heading the business in a certain direction and then realise that it was the wrong business logic and have to redo it. I found that, because we generally have lower salaries in Myanmar, it allows you to have a longer runway. In Singapore, a 10-person team could cost the equivalent of a 70-person team here.

What Next?

Flymya's next big challenge for growth would be to extend credit to retailers to promote sales on its platform. Mike explained,

That's why we're improving our software as we digitalise further. We're going to have more data about the financial strength of the retailers once they start to use our machines and our app, to also run day-to-day POS. If we have the big data of their revenue, we will be in a better position to finance them. These are things that we have to build step by step, and experience and a track record will be important to informing our decisions.

On the flip side, Mike recognises that being an online business comes with its benefits and threats.

Online travel is less complicated than food or e-commerce because it is a purely digital product that does not require logistics fulfilment. But it also means that as an Internet-based business, there are no contractual agreements with customers and no barriers to entry to competitors coming from anywhere. As much as it is rosy, it is also scary. Especially when someone has the financial resources, they can hit you from many directions. They can spend vast resources in R&D and leapfrog your technology, or make investments in customer acquisition that you may not be able to keep up with.

I figured that global players would not come regionally. They plan globally and would probably not connect to the local payment gateways or give local support. What keeps me up at night and prevents the team from becoming complacent is regional competition. We don't have the financial muscle like some of them, but we still have to compete.

Mike's ultimate vision is clear — he wants Flymya to be a serious regional player. 'In the travel business, there is no sunset; the market will grow increasingly larger.'

In 2018, Flymya set up its Cambodia office. Commented Mike,

There are many airlines in Cambodia too, and they have similar challenges to ours. So Flymya will bring our omnichannel business model to Cambodia to also have a wallet in the country. The amazing thing is that we built our solution for Myanmar, and we are starting to realise that it might apply to quite a lot of countries. Myanmar is definitely a big testing bed. It is a country that we feel that we can leapfrog because we start everything from nothing. It's a blank piece of paper. We can always go in there and innovate.

We are just at the beginning of realising this growth potential, and there is still a long way to go. We have just graduated from kindergarten and there are so many more things to learn. If we get things right, we might very well become the biggest company in the country.

Flymya had innovatively brought the market to the neighbourhood. Begun as a travel portal, and to a large extent still the company's core business, Flymya's technology has enabled local neighbourhood mom-and-pop stores to offer the convenience of local payment for utility, travel and numerous event purchases. As the company expands its services throughout Southeast Asia, its vision is filled with opportunities.

Chapter 11

BLUE OCEAN: GROWING WITH THE COUNTRY WHILE HELPING IT TO PROSPER

Blue Ocean is an inclusive business, and we want to reach a vast number of people, especially in the rural areas. Access to information and financing are absolutely key for the country to grow.

— Htun Htun Naing, CEO, Blue Ocean Operating Management Co. Ltd.

Blue Ocean Operating Management, or BOOM for short, is a group of seven subsidies run by CEO Htun Htun Naing, or Nelson, as he is popularly known. Founded in 2009 as the first call centre in Myanmar, the group now boasts 850 employees and conducts operations throughout the region. The business has also diversified into mobile value-added services, fintech and venture capital for startups. A sort of a hybrid, the company is a profit-seeking operator in several verticals, while also reaching out to the entrepreneurial community to develop an ecosystem for small and medium-sized companies (SMEs) and startups that would enable rural economic growth throughout Myanmar.

Blue Ocean is a company that demonstrates how a business in Myanmar can swim along with the changing tides. Learning how and when to zig and zag through them is not always an exact process. Nelson, who sees himself as a serial entrepreneur, had his share of successes and failures before starting Blue Ocean. Along the way, he kept learning how to adjust to the changing tides and reaped the benefits of being nimble and fast.

A Serial Entrepreneur

Nelson has led many different lives in his career, and commented,

> *From 1993 to 2000, I had worked in marketing and business development for MNCs. I launched Myanmar Beer when working for Tiger Beer, and then I worked at Campbell's. When people drink, they need snacks so they can drink more, so in 2001, I decided to set up my own business selling potato chips.*

Nelson was confident about his ability to sell to the market, and he had all the right connections with beer pub owners. However, it soon dawned on him that producing potato chips was challenging, as he had to deal with matters such as equipment maintenance, frying methods and quality control, not to mention erratic input prices and fragile supply chains. At the other end of the process was the question of how to collect cash and payment from the customer.

Before founding Blue Ocean, Nelson had been a part of eight startup businesses — including one in IT, a trading company, a cybermall and a restaurant — which failed. Because of these experiences, he considered himself a serial entrepreneur. He also learnt many valuable lessons along the way that he subsequently applied to Blue Ocean.

In 2001, I started my own business with seven other friends. There were too many founders. Everyone had an equal vote and everyone wanted to go in a different direction. That did not work out. In my third company there were only three founders, but there were role conflicts among the CEO, COO and CTO... Blue Ocean is 100% owned by me. I don't have to seek consensus.

Blue Ocean

Nelson founded Blue Ocean in 2009. He explained that he had good reason to call his company that as,

Nothing was available in the Myanmar market, and everything was new. So, I was really inspired by the concept of Blue Ocean strategy. Most of my businesses are 'in the blue ocean', where I seized opportunities as I saw them, because nobody was there yet.

Blue Ocean started as a mobile SIM card rental service, based at the international terminal of Yangon airport. At that time, the government was strictly limiting the availability of SIM cards and prices were around US$2,000 each. Nelson believed that, 'Even if the price was a tenth of that at US$200, it would not make sense for tourists to spend that amount for three days of holiday in Myanmar.' Thus, Nelson rented out the SIM cards at US$1 a day. After 2012, when Myanmar started to open up commercially with new telcos setting up, the price of SIM cards came down to only US$1 each. Nelson then wound down the business. 'It was a pretty easy decision. I decided that if I was starting to lose money, I would stop doing that business.'

The next business was fortune-telling and providing football tips via SMS.

In 2011, Blue Ocean started a call centre, a move that eventually became its core business. This was the business that the company would be most known for.

By 2018, Blue Ocean was made up of seven subsidiaries across three verticals, with over 850 employees.

Call Centres

In 2018, the call centre business was Blue Ocean's primary business line. It comprised Burmese-speaking call centres, contact centres and business process outsourcing services. Nelson started Myanmar's very first call centre after visiting call centres in India, Malaysia and the Philippines to see how they operated. In 2003, he had the opportunity to visit one of the biggest call centres in the Philippines. There were 3,000 staff servicing a US customer who had outsourced to them. Reminiscing, he said,

> *I thought to myself, 'Okay, lovely business'! I have great passion for this call centre business because it can create a lot of job opportunities in Myanmar. Most people think that doing business in Myanmar is not easy. Actually, it's even more difficult than you'd think. It takes two years to apply for a call centre permit and to have it approved.*

Because the telecoms industry was protected by the government, operating without a licence could get one thrown into jail. The Myanmar Post and Telecommunication, which was 100% government-owned, was then operating the 100 call-in phone directory hotline. Nelson elaborated,

> *I pitched a suggestion to them, conveying the message, "Why don't you give this business to me? Your staff is impolite and they don't provide good service." And the*

government said, "Yes, go ahead." So I set up the call centre, and I realised that I didn't have even a single customer, and [so] we decided to start with an inquiry service.

Nelson proceeded to set up the 1876 hotline, where people could dial in and ask any question, such as what was showing at the cinema, where they could find a doctor, and recommendations for a good restaurant. The call centre maintained a database on such frequently-queried topics, and would charge a premium to the caller for such answers.

At the time, there were only five million mobile subscribers in Myanmar, and the Internet service was very, very limited. I thought a lot of people needed to access information. So, slowly, I expanded my business to another premium hotline. The first hotline was a phone directory, and general information. The second hotline was for football. Football is one of the biggest sports in Myanmar, so when the football season arrives, people start to ask, 'Hey, who is playing today?' 'Which colours?' and for the game results, of course... And then the most successful hotline is the one for fortune-telling, because Burmese people believe in fortune telling. We employ real fortune-tellers, who will tell you your fortune based on your name and date of birth. And you can ask about your exams, marriage, career, things like that.

Most of Blue Ocean's revenues came from such incoming premium calls, and the revenue was shared with the operator. This business boomed from 2011 to 2014, after which it became less important as a revenue source as more people began to own a smartphone and Internet usage became more widespread. Nelson explained,

The biggest search engine in Myanmar is not Google, but Facebook. We have around 20 million subscribers on

Facebook. If you need to know anything, you just need to check on the person's or company's Facebook page. So, with our directory business declining, I will most likely convert this service into an app. In the future, this business will be 100% digital.

In 2012–2013, as Myanmar opened up, foreign multinational companies started entering the market, and Blue Ocean started its business-to-business services, being the outsourcing provider for foreign companies. 'Local customers like banks and international fast-moving consumer goods (FMCGs) companies such as Unilever started outsourcing their customer care business to us. The call centres are 100% staffed with Burmese-speaking employees,' he said.

Mobile Value-added Services

The second vertical in Blue Ocean after the call centre business was in mobile value-added services, such as SMS lotteries, fortune-telling, health and beauty tips, news updates and motivational quotes. Nelson also prided Blue Ocean on being the pioneer in the market.

We were already engaged with the first government telco since 2010, before the new telecom operators came in. We also grew our market share by including and connecting with all telcos to enable the integrating of phone content and carrier billing, etc.

I see mobile value-added services as a big opportunity. We have 54 million people, with almost 90 percent mobile coverage in the country, and over 84 percent owning smartphones. What we need is useful content for our people. Then, it can work.

Whether you use it or not, mobile internet is there. Even my mom now uses Facebook as a source of information, news and chatting. The thing is, this mobile Internet is the way to growth as a country, but what we need is to provide useful content for our people. The content may be very different from that of our neighbours, but it is about providing whatever content that is necessary.

Investing in Startups

'Blue Ocean is focused on inclusive business, catering to a large number of people, especially in the rural areas,' Nelson said.

Blue Ocean's third vertical was a company called Blue Tech Ventures, which invested in startup companies. Under Blue Tech, there were four subsidiaries.

The first subsidiary was Dr. On Call, which was a 50/50 joint venture with an Indian company that provided telemedicine services to patients from rural areas through call centres, mobile apps and public chat platforms. As a largely rural population inhabits the vast expanse of Myanmar, Nelson commented,

> *Just providing access is a big issue in a country like Myanmar, where you have most of the concentration of doctors in the urban areas, and yet a relatively rural population. Unlike Singapore, where the focus is on efficiency and scheduling, our rural citizens struggle with access.*

The second business was a Fintech company providing a mobile payment gateway, which was another way of leapfrogging existing older technology in a country like Myanmar.

The third business was providing an e-commerce platform for startups and small and medium enterprises, through services such as SaaS (software as a service). One of Blue Ocean's subsidiaries was also partnering with Myanmar Post to provide logistics services for last-mile delivery.

And the final one was an app for farmers. The app provided information assistance to farmers to consult with agri-chemists or agricultural specialists on questions, such as how to increase crop yields, and what are the prevailing prices and potential crop risks that might loom.

Providing Useful Content

In Myanmar, market research and consumer information is in its infancy. So, how does Nelson know the kind of services people want?

> *One is that busy people want things that will help with their daily life. And education is the second. Myanmar is a diverse country and it's a big area, geographically. It's not only the doctors who cannot access the rural areas, even the teachers cannot go there to educate the people. I just returned from a trip to the western part of Myanmar, which is a conflict zone area. I think it's a pity that there are hardly any doctors or teachers there, and they have no electricity. Yet, they have mobile phones. And that is the one asset that they have to improve their lives. We can use this as a means to improve their livelihoods, and to increase their social connections.*

Business Challenges

'In a year, maybe there are two to three months' worth of bumpy days,' said Nelson.

One of the ongoing challenges Blue Ocean faced in Myanmar was the problem of human resources. In a country with a large young population, skill and talent that was employable was still rare. It was common for people to join Blue Ocean, undergo intensive training, and after two years leave for better positions with higher salaries. There was certainly a ready market for people with some experience, thus causing wages to jump upwards fairly quickly. 'You ask any entrepreneur or business in Myanmar, HR is one of the big challenges,' said Nelson.

He saw this phenomenon manifest itself in the call centre business, where turnover rates for employees with six months' experience reached 20 percent to 30 percent. Those who stayed at least a year only saw a 10 percent turnover rate. Nelson explained, 'This is another challenge in part because people think that a call centre job is easy. Then they realise it is challenging and leave. There is a lot of poaching for the middle level and senior management level managers.'

In an environment of wage pressure and regulatory uncertainty, where the price of a SIM card could fall from US$2,000 to US$1 almost overnight, Nelson understood that companies might be wary about taking risks to outsource or spend more than necessary on business services. However, he also identified that there was another group of people that he could help — the entrepreneurs finding their way in the Burmese business landscape.

MYEA

It was with the goal of helping budding Burmese entrepreneurs that Nelson founded the Myanmar Young Entrepreneurs' Association (MYEA) in 2012. It started with less than 200 members, and by 2018, that number has grown to about 1,800. He said,

> MYEA has only two objectives: one is to empower entrepreneurs, and the second is building the ecosystem to help them succeed.

We have a lot of good talent, and many aspiring entrepreneurs who have very good ideas that can go to market. And Myanmar is quite a big potential market. But without the support of an ecosystem, it would be hard for them to grow their business and be successful... We had very bad experiences in startups in the last few decades, because there was nobody, and no ecosystem, who could help entrepreneurs out. The country democratised in 2010, and between 2010 and 2015, things did not change much.

MYEA engaged in a number of different activities that would help in achieving its objectives of enlivening the playing field for startups.

Creating the Ecosystem

The first activity involved creating the ecosystem by gathering new participants, as well as raising the standards of the players.

MYEA is a facilitator. We have investor training to teach the basics of what is investment and equity for example. While this sounds straightforward to the Western investor, here in Myanmar investment is thought of as a loan first and an investment in equity second. For the entrepreneurs, we conduct training on how to pitch a business idea to investors, as well as how to manage their businesses and processes.

We are also building this access to the finance community by engaging the private equity and VCs (venture capitalists). Typically, financing here has been bank-based, which involves collateral. And if entrepreneurs don't borrow from the bank, then they have to look for money from friends and family. Without collateral to back their loan, the interest rate is often too high.

Reflecting on his experiences as an entrepreneur and those he had gathered during this outreach, Nelson observed,

> *Young entrepreneurs are very passionate, but they don't plan their business well, especially for the long term. That includes financial planning. Sometimes they are overconfident and think all that matters is their belief that 'I can do it'. That is why their businesses fail.*

Connecting with Policymakers

Of course, success and failure do not only depend on the entrepreneur's efforts. That is why Nelson reaches out to policymakers in order to see if the rules can be made more favourable for the startup.

> *Some policy changes are needed to promote the growth of entrepreneurship in Myanmar. For example, there is no income floor for tax payment. In Singapore, if the business is not making more than, say, $300,000 a year, you will not need to pay tax. Here, the tax system is quite outdated. We don't mind paying 25 percent tax, but the problem is that the tax laws are not very friendly for business. If your company is just beginning operations, from the second year it is compulsory to pay tax. This is regardless of whether you are making a profit or a loss.*
>
> *Another thing is the lending policies for SMEs. We still need to work with the government to see if SMEs are able to take loans without collateral.*

Enhancing Market Reach

In addition to connecting investors and entrepreneurs and helping them hone their relevant skills, building the ecosystem also included broadening the market reach for products.

People from the northern states do not have access to markets in the southern states. What they do currently is sell to a third party, who then sells to the end party. We are now building the platform to get market access, and the distribution channels, from north to south and east to west.

We need a lot of things for our local market to be self-sufficient, and we are well within our means to cater for the small things and serve the local markets ourselves. But right now, we still need to import simple things such as ball pens, because we are unable to find the right means to get the product to consumers.

Being Inclusive

Nelson's ultimate aim, with Blue Ocean and MYEA, is to be able to help facilitate inclusive businesses and social businesses who could work with the rural population that tended to get left behind when the benefits of business growth and economic development are available. He said,

In the startup community, people are mostly eager to go into tech. But actually, there are a lot of important things that take place outside the tech sphere.

That's why we are encouraging our people, or foreign investors, 'Please focus 50 percent of your business in the rural areas.' Agriculture, manufacturing, green energy, recycling... these are some areas they can look into. The rural market is quite big, but it takes time to build the market; it is a real challenge.

Earned Wisdom

Nelson has experienced many hard-learned lessons from doing business in Myanmar. Through this journey, he has identified a few insights that are key to success in this frontier economy.

I share these learning points with other foreign investors and friends. Number one is patience. Without patience, you cannot be a success in Myanmar, because things can change or be very unstable. You have to keep your reserves and conserve your energy to reach your final destination. And secondly, you need to know where you are going. Without visions and a goal, you can get lost along the way.

Nelson's vision for Blue Ocean is for the company to expand regionally into the Greater Mekong region of Thailand, Cambodia and Laos, in the healthcare, agriculture and education sectors. 'That's the future,' he said.

After eight years, I will become more of a fund investor, to invest in startups that can contribute to the communities. I have one lovely motto, 'Blue Ocean makes things happen.' And if you're a company that wants to make things happen, the biggest enemy you have is time.

Printed in the United States
by Baker & Taylor Publisher Services